THE BINGE EATING
RECOVERY PROJECT

Practical Advice On How To Get Better,
From Someone Who's Been There

Jen Lessel

Manufaktual Publishing

London, United Kingdom

Manufaktual Publishing
c/o Jen Lessel
Unit 20534, PO Box 6945
London, W1A 6US
United Kingdom
www.bingeeatingrecoveryproject.com

Publisher's Note: This book is not intended as a substitute for the medical advice of physicians. The reader should regularly consult a physician in matters relating to his/her health and particularly with respect to any symptoms that may require diagnosis or medical attention.

Book Layout © 2017 BookDesignTemplates.com

The Binge Eating Recovery Project/ Jen Lessel. -- 1st ed.
ISBN 978-1-7913371-1-7

CONTENTS

THE BINGE EATING RECOVERY PROJECT

WHY I'VE WRITTEN THIS BOOK

I cannot remember a time when my eating wasn't considered problematic. It all started with a fateful incident in December 1985. I was three years old and had been given a chocolate advent calendar for the first time. My parents hung it next to my bed in the sunny bedroom with the puppies wallpaper, and patiently — heroically — set out to explain the concept of delayed gratification to a toddler. One piece of chocolate behind each door; one door for each day. Suffice to say I didn't really buy into the concept. The very next morning, my parents found three-year-old me covered from head to toe in chocolate, the ravaged advent calendar discarded by my bed, with not a single door left unopened.

I was, by all accounts, delighted. My parents less so. My mum in particular saw in this seemingly harmless incident the seeds of something darker: A dangerous tendency towards excess; a girl whose appetites were just one small step away from spinning out of control.

Controlling that appetite soon became her full-time job. Food was carefully allocated and monitored. Grandparents were issued with strict instructions to keep an eye on me in case I went looking for forbidden snacks. Friends' parents were asked to give a detailed account of what I had consumed at birthday parties, so my dinner portions could be adjusted accordingly. When I complained or asked why, I was told: *'If you're not careful, you'll end up chubby.'*

This probably makes my mum sound monstrous, so I want to be clear. She wasn't. Not in any way. She was a wonderful mother, who would have done anything for her children. However, like many women of her generation, she also held some highly problematic views about female body image. She didn't seek to control my food out of spite or meanness; she did it out of love and a misguided sense that she was protecting her daughter from the worst fate a woman could suffer: Not being slim.

There was just one problem: Her efforts backfired. The more she — and the wider family — tried to control my eating, the more out of control it got. I went from a normal child with a bit of a sweet tooth to a chronic secret eater, silently stalking kitchens and stuffing snacks under my shirt while no one was looking.

Then, when I hit puberty, I discovered diets. It didn't take long for my secret snacking habit to develop into a full-blown eating disorder. As I went on increasingly restrictive diets, my eating spun out of control. I was regularly clearing out entire cupboards and fridges. Nothing was safe from me. Granulated sugar and dry cake mixes; out-of-date potato salad and family packs of biscuits — I ate it all, and I hated myself for it.

I knew what I was doing wasn't normal, but I just couldn't stop. And the more binged, the more desperate I became to undo the damage. I starved myself. I (unsuccessfully) tried throwing up. I temporarily developed a dependence on laxatives that left me doubled up on the bathroom floor for hours every day. I tried diet after diet after diet. The binges kept on coming, and they kept getting worse. My weight fluctuated so rapidly that I struggled to dress myself. I felt constantly sick and exhausted. During my starvation periods, I was so hungry I was on the edge of hallucination; during my binge periods, I ate so much and so violently that I would pass out.

Even after I left home, the binges stayed with me. It didn't matter that I was no longer a child who had to hide snacks from mum. It didn't matter that I had forgiven my parents for their misguided attempts at controlling my eating. I could rationalise it all I wanted — the habit had become so deeply ingrained, there was nothing I could do to break it.

Not that I was being particularly smart about trying to break it. Although I was now in my twenties and starting to build a promising career, my eating behaviour remained stuck in permanent puberty. I was either on a restrictive diet or binging day and night. There was no in between, no moderation, no normal.

I read countless self-help books and even went for a stint of therapy, but nothing helped. Once the initial buzz of starting a new routine had worn off, I would always end up back in the same place. Alone, surrounded by empty food packets and desperately unhappy.

What Changed

This is the bit where I'm supposed to tell you about the moment that changed everything. The big, amazing breakthrough. But that never happened for me. There was no lightbulb moment. There was no sudden transformation.

And yet, today I am a million miles from the young woman who thought her life would always be defined by her binges. How did that happen? Not through some overnight miracle, but because — after two decades of being in the grip of binge eating — I finally changed tack in my thirties. I finally started questioning the restrictive dieting of my teenage years and began researching and treating my binge eating problem with the seriousness it deserved.

In this book, I am going to share with you what I discovered in the process, the strategies and tactics I ended up using in my recovery, and the lessons I learned along the way. Before we get started, I want to be clear: There are no secrets within these pages. I haven't stumbled across some mind-boggling, never-before-seen trick that will magic away your binge eating. Much of the information and advice in this book you'll have seen before. The problem is you've not been using any of that information and advice to get better. It's all theory; you are not putting into practice what you know. That's precisely the problem I had and the reason I decided to write this book. Despite all the self-help books and guides I read over the years, I couldn't figure out how to actually get better.

I believe a big reason for this is that most self-help books focus on the beginning of the recovery process. Their main aim is to motivate people to take the plunge and get started, but they provide little insight into what happens next. What do you do when the honeymoon period is over, and the initial excitement has worn off? What does recovery look like on a day-to-day basis? How do you maintain momentum over weeks, months and years? And what do you do when setbacks happen? I didn't have a clue and therefore found myself completely unprepared for the reality of recovery. When things didn't click straight away, I got disheartened. When I encountered even a small hiccup, I declared my recovery a failure instead of figuring out how to get back on track.

This book is my attempt at filling in the blanks. I want to give you an insight into what recovery from binge eating looks like in the real world, away from the textbook examples. I want to prepare you for the messiness and frustrations that await you — and give you practical ideas and strategies for how to deal with them. Above all, I want to show you real progress is possible even when your day-to-day reality looks nothing like the neat little examples you see in many self-help books. I gave up way too easily on my recovery attempts because I was always chasing some fantasy concept of what I thought recovery should look like. I wasted an awful lot of time as a result, and I hope my book can help you avoid the mistakes I made.

How To Use This Book

There are three parts to this book. In part one, you are going to **confront the scale of your binge eating problem**, bring your knowledge of binge eating up to speed and learn important recovery skills, including how to use self-help books effectively and how to work with a therapist.

Part two introduces you to the **five pillars of binge eating recovery**. These are the core principles I used to get better. You'll learn why I found them so valuable and try them out yourself using special exercises and worksheets.

Part three is the resources section. Here you'll find the **worksheets**, trackers and checklists you learned about in part two, as well as information on where to get professional help. All the worksheets in part three are also available as free, printable downloads from www.bingeeatingrecoveryproject.com/worksheets

You can use this book on a stand-alone basis, to help you get started and put in place solid fundamentals for your recovery, or alongside a therapist you're seeing, or even another self-help book. It really is up to you. Although I recommend you read my whole book first before making decisions about how to use it (I recommend this for every self-help book, as you'll learn later), I want you to feel empowered to treat it as a tool and reference guide that is there to serve you — and that you are free to use as and how you need it.

A Quick Note On Limitations

While a self-help book based on personal experience can, in many ways, be bolder and freer than more formal books, it also comes with limitations. I want to be clear about those. I have read and researched widely for this book, and I've spent a long time reflecting on what I've lived through and the mistakes I've made but, at the end of the day, my experience is just my experience. I am not claiming universal truths. Not everything in this book is going to resonate with you or work for you. And that's okay. I'm just one person sharing my experience, and there are many other options for you to try.

Crucially, I want to stress that I am not a qualified eating disorder specialist. I can inform, motivate and inspire you, but I can't diagnose or treat you. There will be instances where a self-help book like this isn't enough and you need help from a professional.

In particular, please consider seeking professional guidance if:

- Your binge eating problem is getting rapidly worse
- You are worried about your physical or mental wellbeing
- You feel depressed, hopeless or have thoughts of harming yourself

Binge eating is a serious problem, and there's no shame in asking for help. If you're unsure about where to look for professional treatment and guidance, you can find a list of contacts at the end of this book.

PART ONE:
THE FUNDAMENTALS

TIME TO FACE THE MUSIC

The single biggest step you can take towards recovery is admitting you have a problem. This is true of pretty much anything in life, but it's particularly important when it comes to binge eating. As binge eaters, we are often encouraged to downplay the seriousness of our problem. *You like your food, that's all. Lots of people are struggling to lose weight, no need to make a big deal out of it.*

It has taken decades for the medical and mental health communities to accept binge eating as a genuine eating disorder worthy of serious research and treatment. To this day, medical professionals can be surprisingly ignorant about binge eating, and access to treatment remains challenging. In the media and in popular culture, meanwhile, binge eating either tends to be portrayed as a diet and fitness issue that can be tackled with personal trainers and eating regimes, or as borderline laughable. After all, real eating disorders are meant to make you thin, right? Time and again the message is: Binge eating is a trivial problem that can be fixed with a bit of tough love and self-discipline. *Just put the cake down, love.*

It's little wonder, therefore, that so many binge eaters feel ashamed to admit to anyone (including themselves) they have a problem. Instead we tell ourselves it's no big deal, just a stupid phase, we'll snap out of it; we simply need to pull ourselves together and stop the pity party. We may even feel proud for being tough and not making excuses by dressing up our lack of self-discipline as a 'disorder'.

This kind of thinking — however well-intentioned — is delusional. It is completely out of step with the latest research on disordered eating, which makes very clear that binge eating is a serious problem which requires serious treatment. In fact, since 2013, binge eating disorder has been officially recognised in the Diagnostic and Statistical Manual of Mental Disorders (DSM-5). This doesn't happen to minor dieting quirks that can be sorted with a bit of #fitspo and a juice cleanse.

More importantly, it is entirely at odds with what you're experiencing day to day. You may like to tell yourself your binging is nothing more than a temporary lapse in self-discipline, but **the reality is binge eating is ruining your life**. It's ruining your mental and physical health, your social life and — most likely — your finances. I can say this with a degree of confidence because I lived with binge eating for more than twenty years and it wrecked me. If you're at a stage where you are reading a book about binge eating, I am willing to bet it's wrecking you too.

The good news is binge eating is eminently treatable. Even someone like me, who binged for more than two decades, can find a way out of it and get better. You will be amazed by how much progress you can make. However, you have to face the facts and stop pretending this isn't serious. There's no honour in wishful thinking. You're not being brave by being in denial. You are sabotaging your chances of recovery.

In particular, you need to face up to:

- The long-term **physical risks** associated with binge eating
- The **true scale** of your personal binge eating problem
- Its impact on your **mental health**, **social life** and **finances**

This chapter will help you do precisely that.

Physical Damage

You already know your binges are hurting your body. You can feel it every time your stomach is stretched painfully tight, you're sweating, your pulse is racing and you're so full you can hardly breathe. You know how bloated you are, and how much pain and discomfort you're in. You know about the constipation, the diarrhoea, the heartburn, the swollen tongue, the sore gums and the bad skin. When I say binge eating is physically harmful, I'm unlikely to be telling you anything new. You know what you're doing is bad for you.

Still, there's value in getting a little more specific than a vague sense of 'this is bad for me'. You need to confront the long-term health problems you may end up with. So, let's take a look:

- Stomach rupture
- Type 2 diabetes
- High blood pressure
- High cholesterol
- Heart disease
- Back and joint problems
- Fertility problems

There's a reason major eating disorder charities like BEAT in the UK and NEDA in the US describe binge eating as a **potentially life-threatening** disorder. These aren't minor inconveniences — they're major health problems that could have life-changing consequences for you.

My point isn't to scare you out of binging. If knowing about health risks was scary enough to stop you binge eating, you'd have stopped already. I'd have stopped twenty years ago. I know that's not how it works. My point is: These health risks tell you something important about binge eating. They tell you how serious a problem it is — and therefore how serious you're going to have to be about your recovery.

Take another look at that list of health risks. If you had any one of them in isolation — unrelated to binge eating — I am willing to bet you would seek professional advice, educate yourself, research your options and carefully consider what you should do next. You wouldn't set yourself a thirty-day 'challenge' to get better, jump from treatment to treatment or take advice from random people on the internet. **You would do this properly.**

The same thinking needs to apply to your binge eating. You are going to have to do this properly; there simply is no other way. You need to draw breath, give yourself some space to think and weigh up your options, and then devise a serious strategy that's a match for the serious problem you have.

Mental & Social Damage

Binge eating is not just a risk to your physical health. It also puts your mental wellbeing in jeopardy. Research has shown that binge eaters are at higher risk of developing other mental health conditions, such as depression, anxiety and bipolar disorder. They are also at significantly higher risk of suicide than the average person. But it's not just the big, scary-sounding mental health problems. The small, seemingly insignificant things add up too. Ask yourself:

- How often have you cancelled on friends and family because you worried about eating in public or did not want to be seen?
- How many birthday parties have you missed out on?
- How many nights have you stayed in instead of going out?
- How often have you tried to avoid having your picture taken?
- How often have you eaten in secret?
- How often have you hidden remnants of a binge in a panic?
- And how many times have you said no to sex and intimacy because your body was too broken from a binge?

If you have been binging for a long time, these things may not feel like a big deal anymore. They may just be what you do. So, let me be clear: **None of this is normal.** This is not what a life is supposed to be like. You are not meant to spend your days in hiding. You are not meant to talk yourself out of fun, friends and relationships. Food and eating are not meant to dominate everything you do. You deserve better. And admitting you have a serious problem and seeking proper help for it is the first step towards getting just that.

Financial Damage

Finally, let's talk about the financial cost of your binge eating. After hearing about heart disease and social isolation, this may seem a little glib. Bear with me. In my experience, calculating the financial cost of your binge eating is a surprisingly effective way to confront the scale of your binge eating problem. It's just so brilliantly black and white. You can kid yourself into thinking you won't get health problems or play down the impact on your mental health and social life, but if you're blowing your disposable income on food that money is simply gone.

At various stages of my recovery, I have therefore found it helpful to track how much money I am spending on food to gauge how well I am managing my binge eating. To get you started and spur you into action, however, I recommend you first **calculate your lifetime binge spend**. It's a simple formula:

- Estimate the average amount of money you spend per binge and multiply it by the average number of binges you have every week
- Multiply that figure by 52 to get your annual spend
- Multiply it by the number of years you've been binging for your lifetime spend

Bear in mind you're not looking for something that's mathematically accurate; the goal is to give you a broad indication and help you quantify the scale of your binge eating problem.

In my case, I've worked out I've spent at least £25,000 (or US$37,000) on binge food during my lifetime. I still can't quite believe it even as I type this. That's a car or a deposit on a house or multiple dream holidays. All gone on binges. I'd always felt I didn't have much spending money despite a decent salary, and never understood where it all went. Well, guess what? I was eating my money, quite literally.

That figure shook me up and made me determined to finally take recovery seriously like nothing else. Health risks didn't do it. Mental health and social impact didn't do it. But you can't look at £25,000 and pretend you have a minor problem.

Seeing the financial cost spelled out — those £25,000 wasted — made me so angry. I could have had so much fun with that money. I could have completely transformed my financial security. Instead, I wasted it on something that brought me nothing but misery. To this day, whenever I waver in my resolve, I remind myself of that figure, and it never fails to get me back on focus. I can't get those £25,000 back, but I am going to make absolutely sure I won't waste even more.

———

This first chapter has been all about getting you to confront the scale of your binge eating and realise you are dealing with a serious problem. To an extent, it's been about shocking you into action. However, nothing is going to change unless you are ready and willing to change. This may sound like banal self-help claptrap or the preamble to some big motivational spiel, but it's simple fact. Change doesn't just 'happen'. Binges don't simply stop. Something needs to change in how you think and how you behave. Many of the patterns, habits and coping mechanism you have got used to over months and, perhaps, years, will have to be undone, and new ones will need to be formed.

That's no small feat. In fact, it's going to be exceptionally hard work and require an enormous amount of **self-discipline** from you. But not the kind of self-discipline people tend to talk about in most self-help books. I don't mean sticking to an eating programme. I mean the discipline to expose yourself to new ideas and give them a proper try, even when they make you feel uncomfortable or scared. After all, that is the nature of change. No matter how gentle or incremental, change can't happen unless you allow new ideas into your life.

You will also need to develop self-discipline with regards to managing your own attention span and boredom. I'm sorry to break it to you, but most of the time **recovery is incredibly dull**. It rarely involves transformational fireworks or activities that can, in all seriousness, be described as 'fun'. Instead, it takes months and months (and sometimes years) of slow, hard work and incremental progress.

If all this feels like quite a leap from where you are right now and what you think you are capable of, let me say two things. First, it's totally normal to feel daunted. Recovery is a challenging process, and no one likes being taken out of their comfort zone. Second, there is an enormous range of tools and techniques at your disposal to help you through that process — far more than you probably realise. This book will introduce you to some of them — the ones that I have found particularly useful in my own recovery — but it's far from exhaustive. There are many good books and resources on binge eating recovery available now, and I would encourage you to read as widely as you can. Challenge your own assumptions and seek out new ideas. That way, whenever one thing doesn't work out, you already know there are plenty of other alternatives to try.

EDUCATE YOURSELF

When I finally started taking my binge eating problem seriously and began my recovery in earnest, I was surprised to find how little I knew about binge eating. Over the course of twenty years I had spent endless hours thinking about food and agonising over my binging, and yet I had accumulated very little tangible insight or knowledge. I hadn't educated myself on the causes of binge eating, I didn't know what treatment options were available or how credible and effective they were, and for a long time I wasn't even aware something called binge eating disorder existed. In short, I was largely ignorant — partly because I chose to be ignorant. Although binge eating was making my life a misery, I didn't want to admit I had a problem, so I didn't bother educating myself.

That was a big mistake. My ignorance cost me lots of time and money because I ended up following idiotic advice and listening to snake oil merchants. Time and again I fell for total BS. I don't want you to be in that same situation, so over the next few pages I'm going to put you through Binge Eating 101, including:

- What is binge eating?
- What is binge eating disorder?
- What are the signs and symptoms?
- What causes binge eating?
- What are the treatment options?

What Is Binge Eating?

Binge eating (sometimes also called compulsive overeating) involves eating unusually large quantities of food in a short period of time. This is accompanied by one or several of the following signs:

- Eating very quickly
- A sense of loss of control
- Feeling as if on autopilot
- Feeling dazed
- Eating until in physical discomfort or pain
- Eating despite being already full or not feeling hungry
- Eating in secret
- Eating while distracted or doing other activities (e.g. walking)
- Feeling guilty, ashamed or depressed afterwards

In contrast to bulimia, where binges are followed by purges (typically through vomiting or laxative abuse), binge eaters do not typically purge.

There is no official definition for how large the quantities need to be in order to qualify as a binge or what exactly 'a short period of time' is. I have seen some therapists and coaches talk about 3,000 calories as a typical binge size, but that's anecdotal evidence only and open to debate. The important point is that we're not talking about having an extra helping of dessert or two chocolate bars instead of one; neither are we talking about regular overeating throughout the day. Binge eating involves amounts of food that are much larger than what most people would consider normal, and the binges take place in a relatively condensed time window (for example one or two hours).

What Is Binge Eating Disorder?

When someone binges on a regular basis (typically defined as at least once a week for three months), they may suffer from binge eating disorder (BED). A BED diagnosis will take into account how often a person binges as well as the impact of the binges on their overall mental health, among other factors. This book can't tell you if you have binge eating disorder or some other form of binge eating problem; only a qualified professional will be able to give you a definitive diagnosis. That's why I use the more generic term 'binge eating problem' instead of binge eating disorder. In practice, I don't believe the terminology makes much difference to your recovery options, but I want to be clear I am not offering a BED diagnosis here.

Binge eating disorder was officially recognised as an eating disorder in 2013, putting it on a par with anorexia and bulimia, when it was added to the Diagnostic and Statistical Manual of Mental Disorders (DSM-5) of the American Psychiatric Association. This was an important moment, as formal recognition tends to increase awareness in the medical community and means people with binge eating problems are now more likely to be referred to a mental health professional if they seek advice from their family doctor or general practitioner.

Official eating disorder status also means BED is more likely to be of interest to academics and researchers (and they'll find it easier to get funding), which in turn should lead to better treatment options in the future. This can't come soon enough: Although BED was only recently recognised as an eating disorder, it is already considered the most common of all eating disorders, affecting people of all genders, ages, races and ethnic groups.

What Are The Signs & Symptoms?

You know about the food binges. They are the most obvious and best-known sign of a binge eating problem. However, there's more to binge eating than eating large amounts of food. Two other signs in particular are worth highlighting:

- Extreme preoccupation with food
- Extreme concern about body weight and shape

Binge eaters tend to be **unusually interested in food.** They spend far more time than most people thinking, reading and talking about food, eating, diets and related subjects. For some binge eaters, this manifests itself in constant worrying about what they've just eaten, whether they ate the right foods or the right amount, what they're going to eat next, if they're going to binge, what they are going to eat if they'll binge, and so on. For others, it can mean actively cultivating interests or seeking out hobbies and past times (sometimes even occupations) to do with food. This could include cooking for others, watching food shows on TV, spending lots of time researching recipes or looking at food pictures on social media, devising complex diet plans and eating regimens, or learning about food ethics, sustainability, sourcing and welfare standards.

These are perfectly valid interests and activities for most people, of course, but for binge eaters they can indicate an unhealthy obsession with all things food. Creating more mental space away from food is therefore an important aspect of binge eating recovery. (You'll learn more about this later.)

Another important sign to be aware of is a tendency to be **unusually worried about body shape and weight.** The emphasis here is on *unusually*. Most people are concerned about their size and weight to some extent; lots of people would like to lose weight or change some aspect of their body. Unfortunately, that's the reality of the diet culture that surrounds us. What makes binge eaters different is how much importance they place on body size and weight compared with other people. It's not a small consideration or a minor dissatisfaction. Binge eaters' sense of self-worth, happiness and general achievement in life is completely intertwined with their body image. Losing weight is often the most important goal they feel they need to pursue, and happiness won't be possible if they don't manage to change their body.

This kind of thinking is something binge eating has in common with other eating disorders, and the actual size and weight of the person is irrelevant. Although many binge eaters gain weight as a result of their binges (myself included), not all are medically overweight. Poor body image and obsession with weight loss can happen to people who are a 'normal' weight.

When you plan your own recovery later, it's therefore important you look for strategies that aren't just focused on regulating your eating but address all three key signs of binge eating: The food binges, the obsessive thoughts about food and the poor body image.

What Causes Binge Eating?

This is a tricky question. The short answer is: No one is entirely sure at this stage. As binge eating disorder was only formally recognised in 2013, there hasn't been an awful lot of scientific and academic research to date. Right now, there are several different — and at times contradictory — theories to explain what might cause binge eating, including:

- Genetics
- Traumatic childhood events or a history of abuse
- Extreme dieting
- Depression
- Substance abuse
- Experience of body shaming or bullying

For some people all these factors may play a part in why they develop binge eating problems; for others it might just be one or even none at all. The two main points for you to take away are:

- There are still lots of unanswered questions about binge eating
- It's likely that multiple factors play a role

So, whenever some self-appointed binge eating 'expert' claims to have identified THE ONE THING that is causing you to binge (*Sugar! Carbs! Body hate!*) it's a good idea to be sceptical. They're probably overstating their case.

Having said this, there is broad agreement on one key point: Food restriction (aka dieting) is a factor for most binge eaters. It may not be the only factor, but it plays a role in most cases. That is why credible coaches, therapists and self-help programmes will tell you to stop restricting and dieting while you are working on your recovery from binge eating. And it's why you should be wary of anyone who recommends a diet to you — as a binge eater, restriction is highly likely to harm you.

Why Diets Are So Damaging

Let's start by quickly running through the fundamentals of weight loss. Weight loss happens when your body burns more calories than you're taking in. This is known as a caloric deficit, and creating one requires you to restrict your eating in some way. (Theoretically, you can go into caloric deficit by increasing your physical activity while keeping your eating the same, but most people vastly underestimate just how much extra activity would be needed to achieve this. Therefore, in 99.9% of cases, losing weight requires restricting your food intake.)

Being in a caloric deficit isn't much fun, which is why people look for strategies to make the process more manageable. Enter the diet. Diets are, in essence, strategies to help people achieve a caloric deficit. Those strategies can involve restriction in different ways. Some diets focus primarily on restricting the amount of food you consume, for example through counting calories or macros. Others restrict the types of food you eat, such as low-fat, low-carb, paleo or keto diets. Others still restrict when you eat, for example intermittent fasting, 5:2 dieting, 'no food after 7pm' rules or similar. Whatever it is, the ultimate goal remains the same: Restricting intake enough to create a caloric deficit. Because without the deficit, there's no weight loss. How you achieve that deficit doesn't matter. You could lose weight eating nothing but cake, provided the amount you eat puts you in a caloric deficit.

Restriction, as we've seen, is an integral part of weight loss. The problem is, it's also a huge trigger for binge eating. Pretty much all binge eating experts agree on this, even if they disagree considerably in other areas. What makes restriction so problematic are several physiological and psychological factors. It begins with a powerful survival instinct. Your body has, over the course of millennia, been programmed to protect you from starving to death. It sees a caloric deficit as dangerous. *Food is scarce! You're starving!* If you're consistently eating less than you need (i.e., you're in a deficit because you want to lose weight), sooner or later your body will go into panic mode and try to force you to take in more food. You'll experience this as a strong urge to eat.

Initially you might be able to resist this urge through willpower, but the longer your body believes you're in danger of starving, the stronger the urge will become. Similarly, the stricter the diet and the more aggressive the deficit, the quicker your body will try to fight back by giving you strong eating urges. At some point, these will overwhelm you and you'll do what your body wants — eat so the deficit is eradicated.

This urge to eat in response to restriction is not unique to binge eaters. It's what happens to most people when they try to lose weight. They go on a diet, they experience urges, they work hard to keep the urges in check, but at some point the urges overwhelm them. They break the diet and come out of deficit, often by eating larger-than-usual amounts of food, and may even end up heavier than they started.

For the average person this experience is disappointing, but ultimately they move on with their life. Perhaps they'll try another diet in a few months' time and see if they have more success then. The worst-case scenario is they become a bit of a yo-yo dieter.

For someone with binge eating tendencies, however, it's a catastrophe. That's because binge eaters tend to put much more importance on body size and weight than 'normal' people. They spend more time than average thinking about their weight, and they are much more likely to see their happiness and success in life as linked to the way their body looks. A failed weight loss attempt therefore isn't a minor blip; it's a crushing defeat that feels life-ruining.

This is the psychological fuel that sets the binge eating wheels in motion. Because now a second powerful urge comes into play: The urge to lose weight at all cost. This urge is what makes a binge eater jump right back into dieting after a binge. They restrict food to create a deficit, and soon enough alarm bells start going off in their body once more. *We're starving again! We need food — now!* No prizes for guessing what happens next. This is how you end up in what is called a diet-binge cycle, where you are constantly either on a diet or in a binge phase.

The important thing to realise is this only happens because **both physiological and psychological urges** are present. Someone who goes on a diet and ends up overeating or binging but doesn't have a crippling psychological need to lose weight won't experience the urge to keep restricting their food. Someone who hates their body but doesn't ever restrict their food won't experience the physical urge to binge.

It's the combination of the urge to eat (caused by restriction) and the urge to lose weight (through restriction) that creates the toxic feedback loop of binge eating.

Other Factors

What I've just described is the most commonly accepted explanation for how binge eating starts for most people: Poor body image coupled with restrictive dieting.

However, there are other theories and factors that can explain how binge eating patterns develop. For example, some researchers have found a possible genetic component that could make certain people more prone to developing binge eating. Similarly, a predisposition towards certain mental health problems, such as anxiety or depression, may place some people at greater risk of having a binge eating problem.

Other theories focus on the psychological root causes that contribute to binge eating. These can include childhood trauma or abuse; experiences of body shaming and weight stigma; and problematic role models in the family (such parents who were unhappy with their own weight and frequently engaged in diet talk). Wider diet culture and societal pressures to conform to specific standards of beauty can, of course, also play a role.

Some people find it illuminating to trace their body image and self-esteem issues back to specific events or to contextualise them in this way, and this kind of analysis can end up being a very useful component of their binge eating recovery. For others (myself included) it's interesting but not that useful in practice. As I explained in the introduction, I understood my mum's body image issues played a role in my binge eating, but that knowledge alone didn't help me do anything about it.

Crucially, those other theories still assume food restriction plays a role in the vast majority of cases. That is to say, someone with a genetic predisposition for binge eating would not go on to develop binge eating if they never restricted their food intake — i.e., if they never went on a diet. And someone who suffered weight stigma would not go on to start binging if they didn't also try to restrict their food intake first. No matter which way you look at it, restriction is the common factor in almost every explanatory model around binge eating. Therefore, any credible attempt at recovery must tackle food restriction as a matter of priority.

Stress & Emotional Eating

Stress can be a significant factor in binge eating. It can amplify the urge to eat and heighten the distress you feel after a binge. If you are restricting, stressful events can often be what causes you to give in to your eating urges and fall off the dieting wagon. That is why a lot of binge eating recovery programmes include an element of stress management.

However, while stress can be a factor in binge eating, it is not typically a *cause* of it. This is an important distinction. The relationship between stress and binging is more complex than a simple case of cause and effect. Everyone experiences stress and negative emotions at times, but not everyone seeks relief through binge eating. The fact that you are turning to food as your stress reliever of choice is likely to be rooted in some of the other factors we've just discussed — above all, a history of restriction.

One possible explanation as to why binge eaters use food as a coping mechanism for stress and negative emotions is that dieting has conditioned them, over years, to experience uncontrolled eating as the ultimate stress reliever. This is partly because binge eaters tend to binge on high-sugar, high-fat foods that are very palatable and pleasurable. Eating these foods feels nice, especially in the early stages of a binge. Plus, binging can feel like it's relieving a lot of psychological stress. It's only temporary, of course, but many binge eaters will recognise the sheer emotional relief when you don't have to hold it together anymore, when you no longer have to think about avoiding a binge, when you can just let go.

The final factor that could explain why so many binge eaters use binging for stress relief is, to put it bluntly, because it's the only thing they know. I've already briefly mentioned that people with binge eating problems tend to get incredibly wrapped up in thinking about food and eating. If all you do is think about food, guess what's going to be the first thing you turn to when you encounter a stressful situation? Yup, it's probably going to be food.

This is one of the reasons why I believe a crucial part of binge eating recovery involves cutting down on the amount of time you think about food and weight, and cultivating other interests. That way, over time, you will have a wider range of tools at your disposal when dealing with stress and won't feel like you need to resort to food all the time. More on how to do that later.

Is Binge Eating A Form Of Food Addiction?

'Food addiction' is a term that is sometimes used to describe binge eating problems. There are support groups dedicated to helping people with food addiction (such as Food Addicts Anonymous), some scientists have proposed 'food addiction' could be a form of binge eating disorder, and there is even a food addiction questionnaire — the Yale Food Addiction Scale — that is used to diagnose addictive food patterns.

But not everyone agrees. Despite how widely it's used, 'food addiction' is a highly controversial concept that many binge eating experts feel uncomfortable with. There are three main reasons for this:

- The clinical definition of 'addiction'
- Disagreement over whether it's valid to describe certain foods or food groups as 'addictive'
- And the psychological impact of telling someone they are addicted to food

Let's start by taking a look at the term 'addiction'. Although it is used in everyday language to describe all sorts of behaviours, obsessions and passions — think beauty addict, Netflix addict, gaming addict and so forth — addiction means something more specific in a medical context. Addiction is a chronic brain disorder that affects the brain's reward system in a way that makes it much harder — and in some cases impossible — for sufferers to control their impulses. It has long been established that substances like alcohol and hard drugs can bring about the brain changes that result in addiction, but scientists disagree over whether food can do the same.

Several high-profile studies have suggested that highly palatable foods — particularly those high in sugar — may be addictive in a similar way to drugs and alcohol. For example, a 2017 study published in the British Journal of Sports Medicine described the refining process used in industrial sugar production as creating 'addictive properties' and warned: *'Consuming sugar produces effects similar to that of cocaine, altering mood, possibly through its ability to induce reward and pleasure, leading to the seeking out of sugar.'* Meanwhile, a 2007 experiment by French scientists claimed that rats preferred drinking super-sweet water full of saccharin to getting an intravenous dose of cocaine, prompting lots of headlines about how sugar and sweeteners are more addictive than hard drugs.

However, these findings are not universally accepted by the scientific community. Some scientists have argued the rat study was misinterpreted and can't tell us much about how addictive sugar really is. Others point out that while eating sugar (and other foods) can be habit-forming, it is wrong to use the term 'addiction' because people don't get withdrawal symptoms as they do with alcohol or drugs.

The upshot is, there is currently no official diagnosis for 'food addiction' or agreement on whether it even exists, though this may change in future if more evidence comes to light.

Food vs Eating Addiction

While the jury is still out on whether individual foods can be addictive, there is growing support for the idea of 'eating addiction'. The key difference here is that what people are addicted to is not specific foods or ingredients like sugar, but the act of eating itself. In 2012, a group of European scientists published a study about 'eating addiction', which they described as a set of **compulsive behaviours around food** rather than a substance addiction to food itself. Binge eating disorder could potentially be explained as a form of 'eating addiction', this study suggested, though more research needs to be done.

In any case, shifting from 'food addiction' to 'eating addiction' could help address some experts' concerns about the psychological impact of talking about being addicted to food. Thinking of certain foods as 'addictive' shifts the responsibility away from the individual and makes the problem all about the food and not the person eating it, they fear. As with trigger foods (see below), this can lead to a self-fulfilling prophecy, where binge eaters convince themselves they will inevitably binge if they eat certain 'addictive' foods.

For now, while there is no scientific consensus around whether food addiction exists or how useful a concept it might be in the treatment of binge eating problems, it's best to approach any recovery methods, coaches or self-help books that promise to cure you of your food addiction with a degree of caution.

Understanding Triggers

'Triggers' are something you will come across a lot when reading about binge eating and binge eating recovery. People may describe certain foods as 'triggering' to them, by which they typically mean eating those foods causes them to binge. Or they may talk about how certain emotions or situations trigger binge eating episodes, such as being alone, feeling sad or experiencing stress at work. Although triggers feature in lots of conversations about binge eating, the concept is not without controversy. In fact, experts disagree over how big a role triggers play in binge eating — and some even question whether triggers exist at all.

Much of this is tied to the debate about food addiction that we touched on in the previous section. When some people talk of 'trigger foods', they mean these foods are inherently triggering because of their ingredients or composition. They're high in sugar, carbs or fat, for example, or heavily processed, and this is what makes them uniquely triggering. According to this theory, a person who is sensitive to these kinds of foods and triggered by them will inevitably binge if they consume even a small amount. One bite of chocolate, cake or pizza, and things spiral out of control. The only way to break out of the binge cycle is abstinence — cutting trigger foods out of the diet completely.

Not everyone agrees with this idea. Some experts argue it's not the foods that are triggering, but our attitude towards them. If you have a long history of dieting and trying to avoid 'bad' foods, then you may well find yourself triggered by the smallest piece of chocolate — not because of anything in the actual chocolate, but because you've told yourself you're not allowed to have it. Once you change your attitude, your supposed trigger foods stop having power over you. Instead of cutting foods out of your diet, self-help programmes that follow this philosophy will therefore encourage you to regularly eat 'bad' or 'forbidden' foods, so you can develop a more relaxed attitude towards them. No food should be out of bounds with this approach, and none should be thought of as a trigger.

Emotional & Situational Triggers

The third way to look at triggers is to move the debate away from specific foods and instead look at which emotions and circumstances tend to trigger binge eating episodes for you. Most notably, this can include stress, which — as mentioned previously — is a significant factor in binge eating for many people. Anxiety and hormonal changes, such as PMT, can also play a part in triggering binges, as can simply having the opportunity to binge.

This is something I experienced a lot during my own binge eating history. Back in the day, I used to have lots of trigger foods. Cakes, cookies, sandwiches, ice cream, chocolate bars, gummy bears, bread — these foods were my own personal kryptonite. Or so I thought. Because when I didn't have the opportunity to binge, these foods had absolutely zero power over me. I would go out with friends or attend functions for work and eat trigger foods, and nothing at all would happen. When I couldn't act on my urges, a piece of bread was just a piece of bread, not some all-powerful trigger carb.

If I was in a situation where I could allow a binge to happen, however, suddenly the urge from those trigger foods felt overwhelming. Yet the food itself hadn't changed at all. A piece of bread was still, fundamentally, a piece of bread.

This is why I have found thinking about situational and emotional triggers much more productive than thinking about trigger foods. Looking analytically at my binge eating patterns and using tools such as the reverse-engineering exercise to identify when I typically had my binge eating episodes, and under what circumstances, did far more for my recovery than trying to avoid specific foods.

Your experience may be different, of course. The key point to understand is there isn't just one way of looking at triggers. Committing to abstinence from supposed trigger foods isn't a prerequisite for recovery and, in fact, could even be harmful. If you are working with a coach or self-help programme that is heavily focused on avoiding trigger foods and it's not working for you, know you have other options.

What Treatment Options Are Available?

With the symptoms and causes of binge eating covered, let's take a look at the most common treatment options. We'll cover four categories:

- Psychotherapy & counselling
- Group therapy
- Self-help
- Medication

As with everything you read in this book, my goal is not to recommend a specific course of treatment to you. That's a choice only you can make, ideally supported by medical or mental health professionals you trust. I simply want to make sure you know what your options are. Being well-informed is a real advantage when seeking treatment for binge eating problems. As I mentioned earlier, binge eating is only starting to be recognised by the medical community and you may find that your doctor is not yet up to speed on treatment options. If that's the case, you want to be able to ask specific, well-directed questions to make sure you get the treatment you need.

There's another important reason. Put simply, we owe it to ourselves to be educated about our condition and what can be done to treat it. You don't want to be jumping into nutritional therapy because that's the only thing you've heard of. You don't want to spend money on a course of cognitive behavioural therapy when another type of therapy may be a better fit for you. And, most importantly, you don't want to feel like you've exhausted all your options when you haven't even scratched the surface. The next few pages will show you that **you have lots of options** and, as research into binge eating increases, you are likely to have even more in the future.

Psychotherapy & Counselling

Here's a quick overview of the four types of psychotherapy that are commonly used to treat binge eating problems:

- **Cognitive behavioural therapy (CBT):** Structured talking sessions with a mental health professional to help you identify negative thought patterns and behaviours, and create practical strategies for overcoming them. The focus is on the here and now and how you can change your behaviour in the present rather than analysing what's happened in the past.

- **Interpersonal therapy (IPT):** One-on-one sessions with a therapist to explore how your interactions and relationships with others are affecting your mood and eating behaviours. This could involve dealing with unresolved grief, dramatic life changes, bad relationships or social isolation. IPT is often used to help people who are suffering from depression; a special form of IPT adapted for eating disorders is sometimes referred to as IPT-ED.

- **Dialectical behaviour therapy (DBT):** In-person sessions with a therapist to improve your coping skills when faced with challenging situations and triggers. DBT takes aspects of CBT and often combines them with practices such as mindfulness or Zen to help you better regulate your emotions. A lot of focus is put on avoiding extremes (such as either being on a super-strict diet or completely falling off the wagon) and finding a sustainable middle ground.

- **Family-based therapy (FBT):** Therapy sessions involving you and members of your family with the goal of helping them better understand your binge eating problems and how to support you in your recovery. FBT can also help to identify and resolve dysfunctional relationships between family members that could be contributing to binge eating. FBT has historically been used mainly for kids and teenagers, but is now increasingly being considered for adults too.

Psychotherapy is a specialist field, and CBT, IPT, DBT or FBT sessions should only be offered by a **qualified mental health professional**. If you are exploring psychotherapy as an option, ask your doctor for a referral or advice on how to find a trusted therapist in your area. For more information on how to pick the right therapist or counsellor for you, see the dedicated chapter later in this book.

Which Therapy Is Most Effective?

All four therapy forms described just now have evidence backing them and have been shown to be effective for people with binge eating problems. That doesn't mean they will all work for you, though — or indeed that any of them will. It's impossible to predict how well you might respond to a particular form of therapy or therapist. Personal likes and dislikes can play a big part in how effective psychotherapy is. If you don't like your counsellor, it's hard to fully commit to your sessions with him or her. (More on what to do when this happens on later.) However, an experienced mental health professional will be able to assess you and give guidance on which type of therapy is most likely to work for you.

There isn't a lot of research about psychotherapy and binge eating, but based on current scientific evidence **cognitive behavioural therapy** (CBT) appears to be especially effective for people with binge eating problems. In particular, a special form of CBT that has been adapted for those with binge eating and bulimia problems, called Enhanced CBT or CBT-E, is producing encouraging (though far from perfect) results. That's not a guarantee of success, of course, but it gives you a starting point if you are in a position to get psychotherapy through your health service or insurance provider — or if you have the money to pay for private treatment. Because that's the big drawback when it comes to therapy and counselling: There's limited availability, waiting lists can be long and private sessions are often expensive.

If in-person therapy and counselling are out of the question for you, don't worry. There are some fantastic self-help options available now, including books based on the same CBT principles that have proved effective in face-to-face counselling. I have pulled together more information about self-help later in this book.

Coaching & Nutrition Counselling

In addition to psychotherapy through a qualified mental health professional, other types of complementary and alternative counselling and coaching are available that you may find helpful during your recovery. These can include nutrition-focused counselling and guidance as well as more general life coaching to help improve coping skills or mindfulness. Sessions are either conducted in person or through online courses and coaching sessions. Types of coaching and counselling that are offered in connection with binge eating include:

- **Nutritional therapy:** Online or in-person advice on diet and nutrition, often involving food logging and tracking, tailored meal plans and shopping lists, and advice on cooking and food preparation skills.

- **Hypnotherapy:** In-person sessions with a hypnotherapist or self-hypnosis using audiobooks or apps, with the aim of inducing a hypnotic state during which your subconscious can be redirected away from harmful patterns and habits. In some cases, hypnotherapy is offered in conjunction with CBT psychotherapy or using CBT principles.

- **Health, wellness or life coaching:** Online or in-person sessions with a coach to work towards your personal health and wellness goals. Techniques and coaching styles vary widely and depend on the coach's specific qualifications and experience, but can include stress management, coping skills and goal setting. Some life coaches have studied psychology or psychological principles, but they are generally not qualified to offer actual psychological counselling.

Overall, these types of services are **much less strictly regulated** than psychotherapy, which means it can be harder to figure out if someone really is qualified to advise a person with binge eating problems. Similarly, it's much harder — if not impossible — to say how effective these kinds of treatments are. Alternative and complementary therapies haven't been studied to the same extent as psychotherapy, so there isn't enough evidence to say with any degree of certainty whether they work.

Having said this, there are plenty of people who enjoy alternative and complementary therapies and find them helpful. As long as you go into them with your eyes open, don't expect miracles and understand what you're paying for (some of these services can cost a lot of money!) there is nothing wrong with experimenting with non-traditional treatments.

Group Therapy

Group therapy is a form of psychotherapy that is, as the name suggests, conducted in a group as opposed to one-on-one. A mental health professional leads group discussions and provides structured information and advice. There may also be assignments and exercises for you to complete at home. Group size varies but is usually kept below ten participants. In some cases, everyone in the group has binge eating problems; in others you may be grouped together with people suffering from other eating disorders.

Therapy groups usually open up to new members only at specific times, and you may have to undergo detailed psychological assessment before you can join. Unlike with support groups, contact between group members outside group therapy sessions may be discouraged.

One key advantage of group therapy is that it's typically **much more affordable** than individual sessions, and in some cases may even be free. It can also help you better relate to others, gain new ideas and learn from their experiences. Some people also find it easier to 'find their voice' in a group setting than when talking to a therapist on their own. Crucially, group therapy has been shown to be as effective as individual therapy in many cases, making it a viable — and valuable — alternative to one-on-one sessions.

At the same time, it's a format that isn't suitable for everyone. Some people simply don't like the idea of talking about their personal struggles in front of others, and there's no shame saying you don't feel comfortable with group therapy. If you are interested in group therapy be aware that, just as with one-on-one therapy, it can be based on a range of treatment methods, including CBT and DBT, so it's a good idea to ask questions beforehand to know what to expect.

Support Groups

While group therapy involves a mental health professional leading the group and structuring each session, support groups often have a looser, more fluid format. It's generally much easier to join and the emphasis is on group members sharing their experiences and being listened to as opposed to being given a specific therapy programme to follow. Sometimes a mental health professional is present and acts as a facilitator, making sure everyone gets a chance to speak and dealing with any conflict between group members. In other cases, that role is performed by a person from within the group — for example, someone who has successfully stopped binge eating — who may not necessarily have formal qualifications as a therapist.

One of the key functions of support groups is to make you realise **you are not alone with your problem.** Others are going through the exact same struggles, and you can support and learn from each other. This can be incredibly powerful, as binge eaters sometimes spend years or even decades keeping their problem a secret. Being able to finally talk to other people can be enormously liberating and really help with recovery. As with group therapy, support groups are also very affordable and sometimes even free. Plus, contact between members outside of group sessions is usually encouraged, meaning you often gain a valuable support network and even make new friends.

Some support groups are agnostic about treatment methods, while others will be based on a specific philosophy and encourage members to deal with their binge eating using their method. Examples include groups based on the twelve-step addiction system made famous by Alcoholics Anonymous, such as Overeaters Anonymous or Food Addicts In Recovery. These groups can be very effective for some people, but their approach is not without controversy. In particular, concepts like 'food addiction' and the idea of 'abstinence' in the context of eating disorders have been challenged by some scientific experts. Some groups also incorporate religious or spiritual elements, which may not be the right fit for everybody.

As always, the bottom line is: Not all support groups are alike, so do your research and know what you're getting into before you show up.

Online Groups & Forums

If there aren't any suitable support or therapy groups in your area, online support groups and forums can be a great option. The challenge is quality control: There are lots of groups and forums, and not all of them are supervised or facilitated by qualified professionals, or have enough active members to be useful. In the first instance, look for online support groups offered by recognised, independent eating disorder organisations or charities. For example, the British charity BEAT runs several free support groups through its website, including one specifically for binge eating, called Nightingale. The group 'meets' online at a specified time every week and talks for an hour and a half, with discussion led and directed by a mental health professional. In the US, NEDA has free online forums to support people working on their recovery from eating disorders, including binge eating, while in Ireland Bodywhys offers a similar service.

There are many more support groups and forums available through privately run sites, including some that are fee-based. Not all of them will be right for you, so be prepared that it may take a bit of trial and error before you find a group that suits you. Key things to be mindful of, especially when joining privately run forums, are potential commercial conflicts of interest. If a group receives any money from — or has any links to or affiliations with — a commercial organisation, be it a pharmaceuticals company, a coach or a treatment provider, this should always be declared clearly. Should you find that group members or facilitators talk about a specific type of medication or promote a particular therapist or coach (especially if they're very expensive), it's a good idea to be suspicious and investigate further.

Also bear in mind that support groups, forums and chats that aren't supervised or facilitated by a professional can sometimes veer off in unhelpful directions. Niche ideas can get a disproportionate amount of air time or a small number of unusually active members may end up dominating the debate. Occasionally you also get a 'blind leading the blind' effect, where group members (with the very best intentions) post about 'breakthroughs' prematurely or make recommendations to others based on very limited personal experience.

In my view, online support groups and forums are best used as a source of emotional support and companionship rather than for advice or treatment. For that, you are usually better off going to a professional.

Self-Help

Self-help is often the first treatment option recommended to people with binge eating problems. It's easily available, flexible and much more affordable than seeing a coach or therapist. Self-help typically takes the form of books, though increasingly apps and online tools are being developed to support — or even replace — the traditional self-help book. Examples include the Recovery Record app and Rise Up and Recover.

Different books, apps and tools will be based on different treatment philosophies, but what all forms of self-help have in common is that **you are working through the programme by yourself**, in your own time. There is no direct contact with a coach or therapist. This is obviously why self-help is cheaper and more accessible than therapy, but it also creates some limitations. You can't ask questions, for example, and you are generally going to have to do the programme as written, with limited scope to adapt it to your specific needs. On top of that, self-help requires a degree of self-motivation. If you struggle to remain on track with a programme, a regular appointment with a therapist or coach may help you stay more accountable during your recovery.

Another challenge arises from the fact that there are lots of self-help books available on the market, and the quality isn't always great. This is why there is a chapter later in this book with detailed advice on how to pick a self-help book that's right for you.

While there are no guarantees that a particular form of self-help will work for you, it is useful to know that self-help programmes based on cognitive behavioural therapy (CBT) principles are currently the best researched and have the most scientific evidence to back them. *Overcoming Binge Eating* by Christopher Fairburn is the best-known example of a self-help book based on CBT.

Guided Self-Help

'Guided self-help' is a hybrid between self-help and treatment with a therapist. You still work through the programme mostly by yourself, but are **supported through regular telephone calls**, online chats or Skyping sessions with a mental health professional. This type of treatment has been used for depression and anxiety for some time and is increasingly being deployed for eating disorders, including binge eating. Again, it is typically based on CBT principles.

If you think guided self-help could be a good fit for you, ask your doctor about what options are available. Bear in mind that not all national health services and insurance providers will cover you for guided self-help, so you may need to look at privately hiring a therapist or coach. Although not as affordable as pure self-help, this option should still be significantly cheaper than going for in-person counselling. Before you hand over any money, make sure you read the guide on how to find and hire a therapist or coach later in this book.

Medication

In some cases, drugs are prescribed to help people with their binge eating problems. This might be the case if the problem is particularly severe or if self-help and psychotherapy options aren't helping on their own. Which drugs are prescribed for binge eating (and whether they are prescribed at all) depends on where in the world you live, and how medication is approved and regulated in your country. Be aware that not all regulatory authorities, doctors and eating disorder specialists believe that using drugs to treat binge eating is a good idea, or suitable for everyone. Research is still at an early stage and there remain lots of unanswered questions about how effective (and safe) drug-based treatments for binge eaters are.

If medication is being prescribed for binge eating in your country, it will typically be one of the following:

- Antidepressants (such as Prozac, Luvox or Wellbutrin)
- Appetite suppressants (such as Phentermine)
- Anti-epilepsy drugs (such as Topamax)
- Medications used to treat ADHD (such as Vyvanse)

Exactly how these drugs, which were originally developed for different problems, can also help with binge eating isn't always fully understood. Some of them do it by stabilising your mood and making it easier to deal with anxiety, while others primarily improve impulse control or suppress cravings. Of course, all drugs come with risks and potential side effects, so the decision to go on them should never be taken lightly. Make sure you ask your doctor detailed questions about why you are being prescribed a particular drug and how it's supposed to help you, how long you should expect to take it and what levels of improvement are realistic.

Always keep in mind that while drugs can be helpful for some people, **they are not a magic pill** that will 'switch off' your binge eating. They won't work for everyone and are not meant to be used long term or as a standalone treatment. This means if your doctor puts you on medication for your binge eating, you should expect to have to do some form of psychotherapy or counselling (probably CBT) alongside it. I have not used medication as part of my own recovery process, so I can't share first-hand experience, but it's possible to find reviews and personal accounts online. They can't tell you if a drug might be right for you, of course, but can give you some helpful context and ideas for questions to ask your doctor.

One quick note of caution: Eating disorders — including binge eating — are a big business opportunity for the pharma industry. If you are reading reviews online, always check that what you are reading is from a genuinely independent source and not an advertorial paid for by a pharmaceuticals company looking to sell you their products. Watch out for phrases like 'sponsored by', 'in affiliation with' or 'supported by' on articles. It's also a good idea to scroll to the bottom of any website you are visiting to see who is listed as the owner. A quick Google search will tell you if it's a company with a commercial interest in encouraging you to go on medication.

HOW TO TALK TO SOMEONE ABOUT YOUR BINGE EATING

Before we dive into the specifics of the recovery process — and explore the five recovery principles that have helped me personally — it's worth going over a few key skills that are going to help you in your recovery, no matter which techniques or system you ultimately decide to follow. In particular, these skills are:

- How to talk to someone about your binge eating problem
- How to get the most out of a self-help book
- How to work with a therapist
- How to use tracking and journaling to support your recovery

Not all of these will be relevant to you right this second, but it's a good idea for you to know and understand them in broad terms. Read the following chapters with the aim of getting a good, basic grasp of what's involved with all four skills. You can always return to them later, as and when you need them during your recovery.

For now, let's begin by looking at how to **break the silence** and talk to someone about your binge eating. This is one of the most important steps you can take in your recovery, but it's also terrifying. If the thought of talking to someone scares the living daylights out of you, know that you're not alone. Lots of people feel this way. I know I certainly did. It took me years to pluck up the courage and finally talk to a friend about my binges. But I will also tell you this: Although it was scary, I have never regretted that decision. I only wish I had spoken to someone sooner.

Here's why: As long as you're keeping all this in your own head, it's too easy to back out of recovery. It's too easy for you to kid yourself into thinking you don't really have a problem. It's too easy to carry on as you are. Talking to someone makes your problem real. There, you've said it. It's out of your head. Someone else knows now. You can't pretend it's not happening. (Or, at the very least, pretending has just become a whole lot more difficult.) That's why I've written this chapter. I truly believe you need to talk to someone, and I want to give you **practical tips and ideas** for how you can make that prospect a little less terrifying. We'll focus on two groups of people you should consider talking to:

- People you know personally, such as a partner, family member or friend
- Professionals, such as doctors, teachers or eating disorder specialists

First, we'll look at people from your personal circle.

Talking To People You Know

In many ways, I believe this is the more important group of the two. Getting help from professionals is clearly a good idea, but you could potentially get advice through self-help books. A real-life conversation isn't absolutely necessary. When it comes to people from your private life, however, it absolutely is.

One of the reasons it's so important you talk to a partner or someone in your family or circle of friends is so they can step in and help you if things get really bad and spiral out of control. Don't take this lightly or think it wouldn't happen to you. **The mental health impact of binge eating is real.** Binging can take you to some very dark places. You don't want to be in a position where you are having to explain your binge eating for the first time right at the moment when you are in crisis. Lay the groundwork now.

Confiding in someone who sees and talks to you regularly also means it's harder to break off contact when things get bad. A doctor's or therapist's appointment is easily cancelled — your mum's phone calls not so much. The bottom line is: **There should always be someone in your life who knows what's going on.**

So how do you have that all-important conversation? I suggest you work up to it in three stages:

- Identify the right person
- Prepare what you are going to say to them
- Have the actual conversation

Identifying The Right Person

First, know that you only need one person. There is absolutely no need for you to tell the world and its dog about your binge eating. One person is all it takes. You may already have somebody in mind, in which case you can go straight to the preparation stage. If you aren't yet sure who to talk to, the following questions might help:

- **Who do you definitely not want to talk to?** Sometimes it's helpful to start by defining what you don't want. Create a list of the people in your family and circle of friends, and decide who is simply out of the question. Don't worry if this includes your partner or very close family members and friends, but make sure you honour the spirit of the exercise. You eventually want to end up with a shortlist of people you *are* able to talk to, so don't cross *everyone* off your list. This is about establishing priorities and boundaries, not convincing yourself you can't possibly talk to anyone ever.

- **Who do you see on a regular basis?** Ideally, the person you confide in is someone with whom you can have face-to-face contact regularly. A phone call will do in a pinch, but I would advise against anyone you only speak to online. While online chats and forums can be helpful (as discussed earlier), what you need for this is an offline, in-person conversation. You want someone you'd find it hard to avoid in real life.

- **Who is a good listener?** For your purposes, someone who holds lots of strong opinions and enjoys giving advice to others may not be the best fit. You want someone who is prepared to listen without judgment. Just as importantly, you want someone who is willing to give you their full attention when you talk to them. Ask yourself: Is the person good at making eye contact? Do they tend to put away their phone during conversations? These details matter when confiding in someone.

- **Who is discreet?** If you are nervous about people finding out about your binge eating, make sure you pick someone who understands and respects your desire for privacy. This is especially important if you're planning to talk to a family member, as there may be a tacit assumption that your issues will be shared more widely within the family.

- **Who talks a lot about their weight or diets?** Someone who is preoccupied with their own weight, has an exercise regime they like to talk about or simply enjoys reading and thinking about food may not be a great choice. Part of your recovery will involve creating mental space away from food (more on this later) so you want to confide in someone who can support you in that effort instead of creating additional reasons for you to think and talk about food.

As you work through these questions, remember no single person is likely to tick all the boxes. You are probably going to have to compromise on some level. What the questions are meant to help you with is clarify what's important to you. Can you live with a bit of indiscretion between family members or is that a red line? Are you prepared to settle for phone calls because the person is an exceptionally great listener, or would you rather see someone face to face?

Work out what matters to you, then draw up **a shortlist of no more than three people** who match most of what you're looking for. Give yourself a week to think it over, and then make your decision.

Figuring Out What To Say

It can be hard to find the right words in the moment, especially if the stakes are high. A bit of preparation will help calm your nerves and ensure you get across everything you need to say. Start by creating a list of all the points you want to make. You don't necessarily need to bring that list when you have your conversation; the process of writing it alone will help make your thoughts more organised and coherent.

You may also want to **consider sending an email ahead of your conversation**, explaining what you want to talk about and perhaps even including some brief background reading on binge eating. Sending a written note like this to a friend or family member may sound over the top, but it can be a very effective way to communicate information that you may otherwise struggle to explain in person. It's especially helpful if you think the other person doesn't know anything about binge eating and you'd like them to have at least a rough idea before you talk to them face to face. The following prompts will further help you get your thoughts in order and figure out what you want to say.

- **Work out your opening line.** When the moment comes, how exactly will you bring up your binge eating? Starting the conversation is often the hardest bit. If you don't have a plan, it's easy to lose courage before you even get started. Here are some ideas for how you might want to kick off the conversation:

  o *Can I talk to you about something I've been struggling with?*

  o *I've been having some mental health issues I need to talk to you about.*

  o *Something is happening with my eating habits that's worrying me, and I hope I can talk to you about it.*

  o *I have recently realised I have an eating disorder called binge eating. I'd love to talk to you about how it's affecting me and what I'm doing to get better.*

  You may find one of these lines useful, or you might want to come up with something totally different. The key point is: Take some time to think about your opening line in advance, so you're not stuck when the time comes.

- **Describe how binge eating affects you.** You don't have to go into lots of detail. Your friend or family member doesn't need a blow-by-blow account of everything you do when you binge. But they do need to understand the impact your binges are having on you, and why you need their support. Here are some examples of what you could say:

  o *I have found it hard to keep in touch with people because I'm so worried someone might comment on my weight or the food I'm eating.*

    o *When I've been binging a lot, I often feel so uncomfortable and depressed that all I want to do is be by myself and not see anyone.*

    o *I feel like I am being judged for what I'm eating all the time.*

    o *I can feel the damage the binges are causing to my body, and it really scares me.*

    o *I have been stuck in this cycle for such a long time now that I worry I will never get better.*

- **Explain how the other person can help.** Don't be afraid to be specific here. Most people want to help, but they often don't know how to and worry they'll say the wrong thing. Take some time ahead of your conversation to really think about what you would find helpful. Are there words or phrases you find triggering or upsetting, for example, and want to avoid? Do you have a tendency to isolate yourself and need someone who suggests fun things to do? Do you just need someone to listen? If you're stuck, a good starting point is to ask the other person to avoid talking about food, diets and weight. You could say:

    o *It makes me feel uncomfortable when people talk about their weight or going on a diet, so it would be great if I could be certain those topics won't come up when I'm with you.*

    o *I don't want to eat or drink in public at the moment, so I'd rather you didn't ask if I was hungry, suggest we go to a coffee shop or offer me any food when we see each other.*

    o *I've been keeping this a secret for such a long time. I just need to know that I can talk to you and you won't judge me.*

o *I would prefer it if you didn't bring up my binges. I promise I will talk to you about how I'm getting on, but if I don't mention them myself, please don't ask.*

Don't expect the other person to be a mind reader. Tell them what they can do to help you.

- **Be clear that you're not looking for advice.** Your partner, friend or family member is not qualified to give advice on dealing with binge eating. That's what professionals are for. However, they might find it difficult not to try to fix your problem for you. Explain that the best way they can help you is by giving you emotional support rather than suggestions for how not to binge. It's important you're clear on this, otherwise you could end up on the receiving end of lots of well-intentioned but ill-advised chatter about so-and-so who saw this amazing nutritionist and what's-his-face who cut out gluten. If unsolicited advice is offered, be nice but firm:

  o *I know you're trying to help, but I'm working with a therapist/following a self-help programme at the moment and want to concentrate on that. The best way you can support me right now is by...*

- **Let them know what you're doing to get better.** Once someone who cares about you knows about your binge eating and how it's affecting you, they'll probably be very worried. The best way to reassure them is to let them know you are taking steps to get help and recover. Explain where you are getting advice from, whether you've talked to your doctor (or are planning to), which self-help books you are reading, if you are considering support groups or therapy, and mention any self-care regimes or journaling methods you are trying. Don't be tempted to make promises about recovering or say it's no big deal to stop them worrying too much. It *is* a big deal, and they need to know that. Instead, promise them your honesty: You will be truthful about how you're doing, even if it's not always what they want to hear.

Having The Conversation

The moment has arrived. You're about to take a huge step forward in your recovery. If this is the first time you have opened up to anyone, you will probably feel quite nervous right now. Don't let that freak you out. **Nerves are totally normal.** This is a big step, after all. Keep in mind that the conversation you're about to have needs to achieve only one crucial thing: Letting another person know about your binge eating.

It doesn't matter if conversation stalls at times or feels a little awkward. Nor does it matter if you end up forgetting some of the things you've wanted to say, don't explain yourself as well as you'd hoped or even get some things completely wrong. This isn't your only chance to get this right. This won't be the only conversation you'll ever have. Once you have the first one out of the way, the rest will feel much, much easier. Here are some further ideas to help you navigate the conversation and keep things focused and on track:

- **Take a journal or notebook with you** and capture how you're feeling before and after. Speaking to another person about your binge eating will throw up new ideas and questions in your mind. Make sure you have a way of writing them down while they're still fresh in your memory.

- **Be prepared to answer questions.** There's a good chance the person you're talking to hasn't heard of binge eating. Or if they have, what they know might be incorrect or incomplete. Go into the conversation expecting to educate, and don't be offended if you have to explain seemingly obvious concepts. If there is a lot of ground to cover, you might want to consider bringing a book or article on binge eating for the other person to take away and read in their own time.

- **Don't freak out if they say something insensitive.** If someone is ignorant about a subject, the questions they ask and comments they make can come across as grossly insensitive. This will no doubt feel horrible in the moment, but remember they are most likely coming from a lack of knowledge rather than a lack of care. Correct the person and explain why their comment is upsetting to you, and move on. You don't need to put up with people being rude, but you also need to be a little forgiving in the beginning and allow the other person to learn and improve their understanding.

- **Don't forget to listen.** Having this conversation is primarily about what you want to share, but it's not supposed to be a monologue. It's important you stay connected with what the other person has to say. Pay close attention to their reactions and listen carefully to any questions they might have for you. Understand that this situation is probably quite stressful for them too. Learning that a friend or loved one is struggling with a problem they didn't even know they had can make people feel really helpless. Be patient and reassure them that they are helping just by listening and being there for you.

Dealing With Difficult People

Spending a bit of time identifying a suitable person to confide in should hopefully mean you'll end up with someone supportive and understanding. Unfortunately, you cannot exert this level of control with everyone in your life. There will be people (especially in your family, in my experience) who feel entitled to make comments about your eating habits, food choices or weight in a way that can be very upsetting. It's your grandmother commenting on how much weight you've gained or lost the minute you step through the door; it's your aunt wanting to talk to you about her latest diet; it's your mother going on about how much weight she has gained (while you are left wondering what she must be thinking of you.)

In many cases it's because they don't know you have a binge eating problem and simply don't realise how upsetting their comments are; in other cases they may know you have a problem but don't recognise the severity (or don't care).

The standard advice under those circumstances is to confront anyone who isn't supportive of your recovery process and ask them to stop making unhelpful comments — and to walk away and cut them out of your life if they cannot see the error of their ways.

Here's the thing, though. I have family members like that in my life, and confrontation really isn't a practical suggestion. I am not going to start lecturing eighty-year-olds about their body shaming tendencies, no matter how much they drive me mad. (I swear, I could discover a cure for cancer, negotiate peace in the Middle East and become the first person to walk on Mars, and the only thing certain members of my family would care about is whether I lost or gained weight in the process.) Yet I wouldn't consider for a moment cutting off contact with them. Their comments have often upset me — especially in the early days of my recovery journey — but I do love them, and not being able to see them would be a price too high to pay for me personally.

The situation might be different for you, and I don't doubt for a moment that there are circumstances where breaking off contact with toxic family members is what you have to do. But it's not the default option. There are other choices open to you. Most importantly, there are meaningful steps you can take to protect yourself from stupid, unkind comments from your family without having to cross everyone off your Christmas list. Here are my suggestions:

- **Get a sense of perspective:** It's unlikely that every single member of your family is making toxic comments. Don't allow yourself to think in broad, sweeping statements. Who is actually making comments towards you or behaving in an unhelpful way? How often do you have to see them? Do they really play a big enough role in your life for you to care about what they say and think all that much?

- **Identify potential allies:** Insensitive comments often happen across the generational divide. Older family members can feel compelled to talk to you — and about you — as if you're a child, even after you've long grown up. This is very common, so chances are there will be other people in your family closer to your age who are at the receiving end of unhelpful comments themselves. (Perhaps about their career or choice of partner.) Consider talking to them about your binge eating and the comments you have been receiving. Simply having another person to talk to or roll your eyes at over dinner will make you feel less alone.

- **Emotionally distance yourself from insensitive comments:** See them for what they are — a reflection on the person making them, not you. Some people are ignorant. You are generously letting their stupid comments slide for the sake of family unity, and because you know them to be untrue. It might help to capture particularly upsetting comments in your journal and write something like *'not true'* or *'this is not who I am'* next to them.

- **Talk about it — once:** If you had a particularly upsetting encounter, it's important you confide in a friend or family member ally afterwards. However, make sure you talk about that specific situation only once. If you allow yourself to have endless circular conversations about how unsupportive your family members are, you'll only end up feeling worse — without actually achieving anything constructive. Get it off your chest once, and then move on with your life.

Talking To A Professional

While friends and family members can give you emotional support, professionals can give you tangible advice on your recovery and treatment options. Whether it's self-help books, face-to-face therapy, online chats or telephone counselling, you will need to get qualified experts involved in your recovery in some form.

However, getting access to mental health and eating disorder specialists isn't always as straightforward as it should be. Depending on where you live, how your local health system works and the type of insurance cover you have, you may need to get a referral from a doctor before you are able to see a therapist, for example. All this means you are going to have to get comfortable with the idea of talking to strangers about your binge eating.

Where To Start

As a general rule, **start with the most qualified person** you can find. By 'qualified', I mean someone who understands binge eating specifically. Find an independent organisation that advises on eating disorders, such as BEAT in the UK, the National Eating Disorders Association (NEDA) in the US, Bodywhys in Ireland, the National Eating Disorders Information Centre (NEDIC) in Canada or the National Eating Disorders Collaboration (NEDC) in Australia, and speak to one of their advisers first. These organisations all have helplines and online chats that you can use free of charge to get information on what options are available to you — or simply to talk to someone who understands what you're going through. (You can find contact details at the end of the book.)

By going to these organisations first, the risk of coming across someone who has never heard of binge eating is practically zero. People who work for eating disorder charities and organisations know that binge eating is a real condition, it's serious and you deserve help. Even if you subsequently have to talk to someone else who doesn't get it, at least your first experience of seeking help won't have been negative.

I say this because over the years I have come across doctors who were **completely clueless** — and at times downright unhelpful — about binge eating. Don't get me wrong: Not all doctors are like this, and awareness levels are definitely improving now that binge eating is more formally recognised as a condition. If you have a great relationship with a trusted doctor, then absolutely do speak to them first.

But I also believe you need to go into this process with your eyes open, and that means acknowledging that some doctors still aren't great about helping binge eaters. Part of the problem is that the medical system gets doctors to obsess about metrics. Instead of asking how you feel and what help you need, the questions tend to be: How much do you weigh? What's your BMI? How much weight have you put on? How much weight do you need to lose?

It can be upsetting to face a barrage of questions like this, which is why I recommend you start with professionals who are more specialised, such as those working for an eating disorder charity, before you talk to your doctor.

Know What You Want & Ask For It

If you do decide you need to see your doctor to take the next step in your recovery process — for example, to be referred to a therapist or counselling service — make sure you are clear on what you are looking for before you go in to see them. Doctors are often pressed for time, so **being direct and specific about your needs** can mean you get what you want more easily. Here are some examples of what you might want to ask for:

- *I would like to see a cognitive behavioural therapy specialist to help with my binge eating. Can you tell me what services are available in my area and the process for getting a referral?*
- *I am interested in joining a therapy group for my binge eating. Can you put me in touch with some groups in my local area?*
- *I believe I may have binge eating disorder. How can I get a definitive diagnosis?*
- *I understand medication is sometimes used to treat binge eating. I'd like to discuss if it might be a suitable option for me.*

By contrast, the following questions probably wouldn't result in a hugely productive response:

- *Do you know what treatment options are available for binge eating?* (An eating disorder charity or information service is better placed to help with broad questions like this.)
- *What can I do to stop binging?* (This is too broad a question, which no doctor — no matter how well informed — can reasonably answer in a single consultation.)
- *Why do you think I am binging?* (This is the kind of question a therapist might explore over several sessions. It's not something you will get an answer to in a consultation with a doctor.)

Know Where To Draw The Line

If you ever encounter a professional — be it a doctor, nurse or teacher — who doesn't take your binge eating seriously, walk away. It's one thing to have to educate a family member or friend who may not know anything about binge eating; it's quite another to have to do this with someone whose job it is to help people. Don't waste your time and energy. There are lots of well-informed people who know what they're doing and can help you. **You don't have to put up with incompetence.**

Similarly, if you feel you are being pushed in a direction you're not comfortable with — such as towards taking medication, a weight loss programme or a form of therapy you don't like — stand your ground. Politely inform the person what they're suggesting doesn't sound like the right option for you at this point, and that you'll be looking for help elsewhere. Of course, doing this requires a degree of confidence and knowledge, which is why it's so important you take the time to educate yourself about your binge eating condition and the treatment options available. **A well-informed patient is an empowered patient.**

One final piece of advice for dealing with doctors and other healthcare professionals: Be aware that you may be asked to be weighed. It's often standard procedure to record a patient's weight, so if stepping on the scales is likely to be upsetting or triggering to you, talk to your doctor or clinic before you go in to see them.

I have found clinics to be pretty understanding if you call up beforehand, explain that you have an eating disorder that means you find being weighed very distressing, and ask if it's possible for you to be seen without having to weigh in. If they don't allow it, at least you know before you go in.

HOW TO USE SELF-HELP EFFECTIVELY

I am a huge fan of self-help books. I have read dozens of them over the years — on binge eating as well as other subjects — and gained enormously from the experience. At a time when access to mental health services and binge eating therapy remains difficult and private therapists can be hugely expensive, self-help books are a fantastic, affordable resource that allows you to receive advice and guidance from top professionals and learn from the experiences of others.

Although I have also worked with therapists at certain points in my recovery, my biggest breakthroughs came from self-help books and I believe it is entirely possible to recover using only self-help. Indeed, in countries like the UK, self-help is now the main recommended treatment option for binge eating.

Given self-help books can play such an important role in the recovery process, there is surprisingly little guidance available on how to use them effectively, particularly with regards to binge eating. This is unfortunate. Without a strategy, **you can waste lots of time reading self-help books** without ever getting anything useful out of them. You need to have a plan, starting with the following questions:

- What's the mindset you need when working with self-help?

- How do you choose the right book?
- What should the reading process look like?
- How do you implement self-help advice and monitor progress?
- What do you do when the advice isn't working?

Developing The Right Mindset

For me, it always starts with mindset. Your attitude, your commitment and your expectations are among the most important variables that determine whether a book is going to work for you. If your head isn't in the right place, the best book in the world isn't going to help you. Most importantly, you need to be clear about what a self-help book can realistically do for you — and what it can't.

I like to think of recovery as a jigsaw, made up of multiple pieces that need to come together as a whole. Everyone has their own recovery jigsaw that they need to complete in a combination that is unique to them. The challenge for you, as you start out on your recovery journey, is that you have no way of knowing how many pieces there are to your jigsaw, nor do you know in advance how many pieces a particular self-help book is going to give you. Perhaps it will give you ten pieces, perhaps two, perhaps none at all. The only way to find out is by trying out the advice in the book.

The key point to understand is that **no single self-help book will have all the answers**. No single book — no matter how brilliant — will provide you with every single piece you need to complete your recovery jigsaw. You are most likely going to have to read several books to get the information and advice you need — and only *you* can then put together those different pieces and complete your recovery jigsaw. Self-help books can guide you in that effort, but they can't do the job for you. If you expect a book to cure you, you will only end up disappointed.

Marketing Myths

The reason I feel so passionate about the need to develop the right mindset for self-help books is because it made such a difference to my own recovery. Making that shift from hoping a book would fix me to recognising it might have some answers but not all of them was a really important step for me. Suddenly I felt so much less pressure. Once I no longer expected a book to do it all, I could read it much more calmly and rationally. I could concentrate on getting what I needed from the book instead of panicking about whether it was finally going to be the one to 'cure' me.

This is particularly important given how self-help books tend to be marketed. The most common marketing trope used to sell them is that of the all-knowing authority. A renowned expert has written a book to give you the *definitive* take on your problem and the *definitive* way to solve it. Forget about all the other books in the market. This is the last book on binge eating you'll ever need to read!

By pushing this idea, the self-help industry creates unhealthy expectations of what a single book is likely to do for you. The disappointment that inevitably follows can be devastating, so make sure you protect yourself by firmly managing your own expectations.

While we're on the topic of unhelpful self-help marketing tropes, do also keep an eye out for books that are marketed aggressively on their novelty or controversy. Novelty is often used to entice readers, promising a new take, a new angle or a new technique. However, novelty can't tell you if a book is any good. It is not an indication of quality, although it can help create lots of publicity. As a result, poor books with a quirky or interesting new angle sometimes end up getting many more sales and reviews than good books that play it straight.

The same goes for controversial claims or exaggerated promises that take advantage of the fact that many people looking for self-help — binge eaters included — want to believe the dream of the quick fix and the miracle cure.

This is why you are much more likely to find books with titles like *'35 amazing new techniques to help you stop binge eating for good'* than those that emphasise hard work, long-term commitment and consistency. Those things aren't new, controversial or quirky, so they don't lend themselves to punchy marketing slogans. But more often than not it's the boring stuff that works, not the gimmicks.

You Don't Need To Prove Yourself

A self-help book is meant to be a tool that serves you. It needs to prove its usefulness to you — not the other way around. Keep this in mind, as self-help books can occasionally have a weird passive-aggressive undercurrent where recovery success becomes all about whether *you* want it enough, not whether the advice in the book is any good.

It is, of course, entirely true that you are the one who has to change and take action. Your commitment and your attitude are vital components in your recovery. The buck does stop with you, and self-help authors are right to challenge you on your desire to change. However, I always get a little suspicious when books talk a lot about self-discipline and what *you* need to bring to the table. At times, this can be a deflection tactic and a way for authors to hedge against disappointed readers complaining about advice that didn't work for them. *Wasn't the book's fault — you just didn't want it enough!*

The reality is **even good advice doesn't always work for everybody**, and credible authors know and are comfortable with that fact. They don't need to call into question your commitment or self-discipline to protect themselves and their egos.

Choosing The Right Self-Help Book

You are looking for serious advice on a serious problem. Your process for picking a self-help book should reflect this. Don't buy random books just because you've seen them mentioned online. Take your time and do some research.

In particular, **be careful with books that promise dramatic transformations** or quick results as well as anything focused on weight loss or dieting. I would also exercise caution around books that aren't specifically about binge eating but instead talk about 'problem' or 'emotional' eating. In my experience, you want targeted, specialist advice for your binge eating, not some generic catch-all.

On top of this, you should **run at least a basic search on the author**, especially if they are being billed as a high-calibre professional. Don't rely on what it says on the cover blurb or in their author bio. If someone is a world-leading authority in their field, you should be able to find evidence of their qualifications and their clinical or practical experience beyond the book they've written. Tread carefully if someone is a supposed 'guru', but you can't substantiate their credentials.

Being clear about who you're taking advice from is becoming increasingly important because of the rise of self-publishing. I'm a big proponent of self-publishing (this book is self-published) but I do think it presents challenges for the self-help market. The main one is quality control. Once upon a time an author had to persuade a publisher that their book was worth publishing. The publisher would take a view on whether the book idea was commercially attractive and, crucially, whether the author was qualified to write it.

With the advent of self-publishing, this kind of gatekeeping is quickly disappearing. Now, **anyone can publish a book** simply by uploading it onto Amazon or other e-book distributors. Even paperbacks can be created by authors themselves, with the help of so-called print on demand services. It's quick, it's easy and it doesn't cost much money.

This is wonderfully democratising and gives readers access to a much wider range of views and opinions than before, but it also means there is nothing stopping people from publishing absolute garbage. Online book stores are awash with badly written self-published books full of typos and errors.

This is bad enough in a work of fiction, but in a self-help book sloppy research and factual errors can be downright dangerous. That's why it's crucial you do your homework. **Don't ever assume someone is a legitimate expert just because they've published a book.**

One final tip: Take a look at the cover. It always makes me uncomfortable when I see self-help books about binge eating (or disordered eating in general) with cheap stock images of wide-eyed people stuffing junk food into their faces. As someone with a history of binge eating, I find these images tacky and offensive. It would never cross my mind to put something like that on the cover of a book that's meant to help and empower people with an eating disorder. While I appreciate that some authors don't get a say in their covers, it makes me question just how well they — and the publishing company they've worked with — really understand the audience they're writing for.

7 Red Flags To Watch Out For

In addition to checking someone's qualifications, there are some basic red flags you should look out for when picking a self-help book:

- **Red flag 1: It's a diet.** This one's probably the biggest tell-tale sign. Food restriction has been shown, time and time again, to be a contributor to binge eating. An 'expert' who doesn't know this — or doesn't care — and still tries to sell food restriction to people with disordered eating is either dangerously stupid or cynical and exploitative.

- **Red flag 2: Weight loss promises.** A logical extension of the first one, but worth spelling out in its own right because it's so common — and so tempting. Most binge eaters are desperate to lose weight, but weight loss and recovery often aren't compatible goals. They can't be pursued at the same time. (More on this on later.) Any author or coach who claims otherwise doesn't have your best interests at heart or isn't educated enough on binge eating to be taken seriously. In particular, if they have 'before' and 'after' pictures of clients on their website or in their book, take your money and run.

- **Red flag 3: Quick fixes & miracle cures.** Anything that promises you a quick (or easy) solution to a problem as complex and multi-factorial as binge eating isn't credible. There is no quick fix, no single hack or tweak you can use to stop binging overnight. Be wary of anyone who claims they have found the one thing that will fix you. Similarly, steer clear of anyone who promises to help you recover within a set period of time (for example, a six-week course to make you binge-free). There is no way they can know how long it's going to take you to recover, and making these kinds of promises is a bad sign.

- **Red flag 4: Pseudo science.** There is lots of pseudo-science in food and nutrition in general, so it's little wonder dodgy scientific claims creep into discourse about binge eating. Crucially, it's not just scammers and con artists who use pseudo-science to give their BS the look of legitimacy. Well-meaning people can be surprisingly ill-informed about science and end up spouting nonsense despite their best intentions. The most common way you're going to encounter pseudo-science in connection with binge eating is when certain foods or food groups (such as sugar or carbs) are said to have properties that cause binging and therefore need to be avoided. There simply isn't any solid evidence to suggest that's true.

- **Red flag 5: Dogma and absolute truths.** Binge eating and its causes remain poorly understood. It's not always clear which treatments work, and why. Not every type of therapy or self-help is going to work for everyone. Credible professionals know this and are comfortable talking about uncertainty and the limits of their own knowledge. They are happy to acknowledge their approach may not work for everyone. BS merchants, on the other hand, tend to suggest they have found the one, true answer that applies to everyone and don't like to admit there are things they don't know or be challenged on their beliefs.

- **Red flag 6: Conspiracy theories.** *The REAL reason you're still binging. What the medical establishment won't tell you about binge eating disorder. How Big Food is keeping you addicted.* Claims of this nature are a massive red flag. They're a sales trick that exploits our desire to blame some external factor for our problems instead of taking personal responsibility for our recovery. There are, of course, perfectly valid concerns to be raised about, say, the role of the food industry in shaping our eating patterns, but that's not what conspiracy theorists are trying to do. They're trying to convince you there's something secret that's stopping you from getting better, and only they and their special insight can help you (for a hefty fee, naturally).

- **Red flag 7: Shady commercial deals.** Authors and coaches have to make money, and there's no shame if they seek to supplement their income outside of book sales and coaching. The problem is when commercial deals create a conflict of interest that compromises their ability to give good, objective advice and guidance to their clients. For example, if someone endorses a food tracking app, are they really going to speak out about the risks of food tracking to some people? Also, if a binge eating coach or expert endorses a specific food or supplement, you should definitely look elsewhere.

Decoding Reader Reviews

Reader reviews can be useful a tool when deciding whether to buy a book, and I recommend you read them before purchasing. Having said this, they come with limitations you need to be aware of. One of the biggest challenges lies in the nature of self-help itself, particularly for a complex problem like binge eating. The reality is that different people respond to different styles of advice and treatment — sometimes in unpredictable and poorly understood ways — meaning **results can be hugely variable**, even for very good books. *Does this book work?* may sound like a straightforward question, but more often than not there is no clear yes or no answer. It's often a case of 'it depends'.

The problem is that reviews are not very good at giving you a sense of what 'it depends' means. They can't tell you what percentage of readers actually found a book effective because not everyone who read the book will leave a review. All you have to go on is the experience of a small number of self-selecting individuals who decided to write a review.

What complicates this further is the fact that people who do leave reviews tend to give highly positive ratings. In a 2018 study, researchers at Columbia Business School found **82% of books reviewed on Amazon received either a four or five-star rating**.

That's not because those reviews are fake, but because research has shown that people who have an extremely positive experience with a product are much more likely to leave a review than those who have an average or negative experience. If a book isn't that great, most of us simply don't bother reviewing it. (People who really hate a product are also more likely to leave a review than the average, though not nearly as much as those who really loved it.)

This is how you can end up with tons of rave reviews that make a book look like it is miraculously effective for anyone who reads it. Or why you might see lots of glowing reviews for a book that did nothing for you, which then makes you feel like everyone else is having amazing breakthroughs except you. Let's be clear: This isn't the case. Those reviews are not telling the full story. What you are seeing is mainly what a small sample of people who absolutely loved the book thought about it, while everyone else mostly stays silent.

Another limitation arises from *when* people write reviews. My sense from having studied self-help reviews is that lots of them are written soon after the person bought the book. You see very few reviews that talk about someone's experience with a book over the course of several months or even a year. This is problematic because it means you can't tell if a self-help book works long term. It can also tip the scales in favour of books that offer quick fixes. Someone goes on an extreme programme, they see dramatic initial results, they're super happy and write a glowing review, but if the results turn out to be unsustainable that person typically doesn't go back to edit their review to say things didn't work out. What you're left with is a permanent record of their initial enthusiasm as opposed to a sense of whether the book actually proved effective long term.

Having said all of this, I still believe reader reviews are valuable — provided you read them with the right expectations. I don't think there's much point reading reviews to figure out if a book 'works'. Instead, **use reviews to gauge the general quality of a book** and learn about its key themes. Is it well written and free of typographical and factual errors? Is it a slow or quick read? Does it present a compelling argument? Is the author advancing original ideas or is the content derivative? Are there any exercises and practical components to the book?

Those are all perfectly appropriate questions that reviews can help answer. For anything else, you are simply going to have to read it yourself and make up your own mind.

How To Read A Self-Help Book

I believe there is a definite knack to reading self-help books. They're not like other books. They shouldn't be read casually but with a view to extracting the information and advice you need from them. Most importantly, you should **always start by reading the whole book** first. I say this because I used to jump straight into books, desperate to get started with the programme and the exercises, only to find myself out of my depth later on because I had rushed things, skim-read and skipped sections and generally not paid close enough attention.

This caused me to waste lots of time. You can't skim-read your way through what is supposed to be potentially life-changing advice. To get the most out of a self-help book you need to know where the author is going and what their overarching argument is. You need to know exactly what the programme entails, how it is structured, what will be required of you and whether you need to buy anything or prepare equipment. You don't want to start and find out ten chapters in that there's an element to the book you're not comfortable with or don't have the resources to do.

So, set aside some time and read the whole thing cover to cover. Don't rush. Don't skip. Don't read ahead. Don't do any of the exercises yet or take notes. Right now, all you want to do is read and take in what the book has to say. Once you have finished, **take a moment to reflect.** Is this still a book that appeals to you? Do you have confidence in what the author is saying? And do you have the time and resources to follow the programme as described?

It is completely fine for you to decide at this stage that the book isn't right for you. Of course, it's annoying if you've spent money and time on it already, but it's better to pull the plug now than to waste any more time on something you don't fully believe in.

If you are happy to continue, it's time to **read the book for a second time** — this time armed with a pen and notebook. Write down any actions the book requires you to take. You can afford to skim-read during this process as you have already read the book in full. At the end, you should have a list of all the different actions set out in the book, in the order recommended by the author. It's okay for you to **do the exercises** in the book at the same time as you're creating your list, though I sometimes like to leave that for a third read so I can focus on one thing at a time. Go with whatever feels right.

Creating a list of actions achieves two things. First of all, it gets you into an **action-focused mindset.** Recovery is all about doing. You need to be clear on what exactly you are required to do as part of a self-help programme so you don't end up in that weird, unproductive limbo state where you think about how much you're going to change but don't ever take any action. If the actions are written down, it's much easier to see what your path is meant to be.

Second, it helps to engage you with the book on a deeper level and gets you to really understand its structure and arguments. This is very important. As I said right at the start, you are looking for serious, life-changing advice from a self-help book on binge eating, so you need to understand it as thoroughly as you can.

One quick final note on reading: Make time to **re-read self-help books occasionally**, particularly ones that you didn't find helpful first time around. Your recovery needs change over time. A book that didn't do much for you a year ago may now prove useful. You may also find that simply taking a different approach to reading will result in you getting something out of a book you previously thought ineffective. So, don't feel you necessarily have to buy new self-help books. You may have everything you need on your bookshelf already. Sometimes all it takes is a new way of looking at things.

Putting The Book Into Action

This is the point at which you formulate what you want to get out of the book. More specifically, **what you hope to learn** as a result of doing the programme. I don't believe broad outcome-focused goals like *'I want to stop binging'* or *'I want to binge less'* are helpful. Thinking about what you want to *learn* is much more productive.

Do you hope to get a deeper understanding of your binge eating patterns and triggers, for example? Do you want to try out some new stress management techniques and see how they affect your binges? Or do you want to find out whether meal planning could be an effective strategy for you? Whatever it is, make it specific to the book you're reading and capture it in writing. A few sentences will do.

You should also take a moment to write down your thoughts and feelings about the book more generally at this stage. What are you excited to try? Is there anything that worries you or is making you anxious? Write it all down. You will find this useful when reviewing your progress later.

Your next step should be to **implement the book as it is written**. Don't make any tweaks, don't skip bits that don't appeal to you or complete exercises in a different order to what is in the book. Experience the programme as the author intended it. You won't know if a book works for you if you immediately put your own spin on it.

While you are following the book, make sure you have a regular review process to keep track of how it is working for you. I recommend you **have a weekly review session** where you sit down and review which advice from the book you tried that week, and the effect it's had.

There's a template for a weekly review session sheet at the back of the book, which is also available as a download from www.bingeeatingrecoveryproject.com/worksheets

Alternatively, you can simply jot down a few bullet points or loose sentences that capture where you're at with the programme, what you like and don't like, and what's working and not working so far.

What To Do If The Book Isn't Working

You've been following your self-help book by the letter, but things just aren't clicking. No need to panic. Not every self-help book is going to be the right fit for you. Before you give up on a book, however, ask yourself a few questions. Most importantly: **Have you given it enough time?** This is one of the biggest problems people run into with self-help. They expect big changes to happen quickly, and then lose faith.

I know this all too well. I used to throw away self-help books after barely giving them two weeks. What's helped me break out of this habit is what I call the **Thirty Day Rule**. Under that rule, I am not allowed to make changes to a programme or give up on it until I have given it a full thirty days. Thirty days is now the earliest point at which I allow myself to even *consider* whether something may not be working for me. If you haven't yet given your book thirty days, hold your nerve and continue. You're only getting started. It's far too early to draw conclusions.

The second question to ask yourself is: **Have you been following the programme exactly as written?** It's easy to start making a few tweaks here and there, and before you know it you are essentially doing a completely different programme to what is in the book. So, take a step back, look at the list of actions you wrote down right at the start, and hold yourself accountable to doing what is in the actual programme.

The third question you should ask is: **Are your expectations realistic?** In particular, make sure you are not falling into the trap of thinking a binge means the programme isn't working. You will still binge when you start recovery. It's normal. There's no need to freak out. (You'll learn more about how to set realistic expectations for your recovery in the chapter on pragmatism.)

Once you have given a book thirty days, and you're happy that you've followed it as intended and your expectations are realistic, the next step is to **analyse precisely what is and isn't working**. It's very rare to find nothing valuable at all in a book, so don't dismiss the whole thing out of hand. Instead, ask precise questions. What in particular is making you feel like the book isn't working? Was there a trigger or incident? Can you identify a specific aspect of the book or an exercise that isn't working? Look at your review session entries from the past thirty days and see if you can detect any patterns. Challenge yourself to be honest. Are you being rational when you say the book isn't working, or is it that you've had a setback and now you're feeling despondent and want to try something else?

You then need to take a view on whether you can make changes to the programme to address your concerns. **Your first instinct shouldn't be to abandon everything** but to make amendments and tweak things. I'll give you an example. I once followed a very well-respected self-help book on binge eating that taught me a lot. The only problem was that it required weekly weigh-ins. Now, I have always been very anxious about weighing myself, but the author had a compelling rationale for why weigh-ins were important. I wanted to do the programme as written, so I decided to go along with it.

Long story short: I simply could not cope with those weigh-ins. I actually tried them for more than thirty days and weighed myself for a couple of months, but they were just the worst trigger for me. It didn't even matter which direction the scale was moving. If I was heavier than I thought, I would get upset and binge. If I was lighter, I would also binge. What's more, I was constantly anxious and spent hours fretting about the next weigh-in. In the end, I had to pull the plug and accept this was a component of the programme I was simply not going to do.

Some might say that's a bad attitude, that I was cherry-picking and that I deprived myself of an important learning experience. Those are valid concerns, but I also believe you know yourself best. If you have given a programme a fair shot, stuck with it for a decent amount of time, done everything that was asked of you and aren't taking the decision lightly, then you are entitled to take action if something isn't working out for you.

In my case, that was certainly the right decision. I got lots of helpful and practical advice out of that book, which I wouldn't have if I had forced myself to continue with the weigh-ins. It would have got to a point where I would have said 'screw it' and abandoned the whole thing.

Crucially, if you are making changes to a programme, **make sure you have a process for it.** Don't change lots of things all at once. Make one tweak at a time and write down what you're changing, and why. Then give it at least thirty days before you make any further changes. Provided you are conscientious in your decision making, you are perfectly within your rights to make changes to a programme so it better suits your needs.

HOW TO WORK WITH A THERAPIST

Many of the principles we discussed in the chapter on self-help also apply when you are working with a therapist or coach. Just as with self-help books, not every therapist is going to be a good fit for you, and you may need to accept a degree of trial and error as part of the process. However, as therapists and coaches are often expensive (and, depending on where you live, you may have to bear that cost partly or wholly yourself), the stakes are much higher. A bit of money wasted on a self-help book is little more than an annoyance; a big wad of cash spent on months of therapy without anything to show for it is a much bigger problem.

As I don't know where in the world you live, I won't be able to give you specific advice for how to get therapy within your particular country or health system. For the same reason, I won't be able to tell you how much therapy or coaching is going to cost you. What I *can* give you are general principles and questions to ask, which will help you find the right therapist and get your money's worth no matter where you are. So, in this chapter, you will learn:

- How to go about finding a therapist or coach
- What questions to ask to make sure they are a good fit for you

- How to get the most out of the therapy or coaching process
- What to do when things aren't working out

Finding A Therapist Or Coach

Let's start with some important definitions. When I talk about therapists, I mean qualified mental health professionals such as psychologists, psychotherapists, psychiatrists, registered or accredited counsellors, and similar. Therapists with these types of job titles typically had to study to degree level or higher in order to get their qualifications, and will be registered or accredited through major professional bodies. Examples of such bodies include the American Counseling Association (ACA) and the British Association for Counselling and Psychotherapy (BACPR).

Coaches, on the other hand, can come in a wider variety of forms and include eating disorder coaches, lifestyle coaches, diet coaches, body image coaches, etc. Some of these will also have trained with professional bodies, though the qualifications needed to call yourself a coach tend to be significantly lower than those required for therapists.

The third category of professionals you may consider hiring are diet and nutrition specialists, such as dietitians or registered nutritionists. Again, there are lots of accreditation bodies, and standards for nutrition-related jobs vary. In most countries, however, the term 'dietitian' is protected by law, which means standards are stricter.

Which Qualifications Matter?

Qualifications are not a guarantee of success. How much you get out of working with a therapist or coach is as much about personal connection and rapport as it is about formal qualifications. It is entirely possible that a coach with comparatively informal training will be of great help to you, and a high-calibre therapist with a PhD could prove useless.

However, qualifications do **help you to manage risk**. Therapists and coaches can be very expensive —and, crucially, bad ones can hurt you. It makes good sense to try to increase your chances of having a positive experience. In my opinion, this includes opting for someone with formal training, recognised qualifications and plenty of experience.

Unfortunately, establishing someone's qualifications isn't always as easy as it should be. The way job titles around mental health, counselling, coaching and nutrition are regulated is an absolute nightmare. There are lots of different titles, lots of professional and accreditation bodies, and lots of different qualifications and standards. It's incredibly confusing. Two people could have very similar-sounding titles but vastly different qualifications and training.

Let's take a look at nutrition qualifications as a case in point. I'm going to be using examples from the UK, but the situation is similarly confused in other parts of the world. As I mentioned, the term 'dietitian' is regulated by law. To become a dietitian, people study at university for at least three years, including biochemistry and physiology, and are bound by a professional code of ethics. They are also allowed to administer certain prescription-only drugs. The term 'nutritionist', on the other hand, has no legal protection. I could call myself a nutritionist right now and start taking clients, and there'd be no way to stop me. However, to be a 'registered nutritionist' requires certain professional qualifications, including in many cases a university degree, as well as affiliation with a professional body that oversees standards.

It gets more confusing still. There is zero regulation around the terms nutritional therapist and clinical nutritionist — yes, even though it has the word 'clinical' in it. Anyone can call themselves that. The same goes for wellness coaches, body positivity experts or binge eating counsellors. Some therapists choose to voluntarily register with professional bodies and those will typically have higher standards, but it's not a requirement. This doesn't mean coaches with these titles are bad, but it can mean the training they've had was very informal. Some nutrition certs, for example, only last a few weeks, as do certain counselling courses.

This is why it's so important that you do your research on any therapist or coach you are looking to hire. Don't assume someone with an impressive-sounding job title has impressive credentials. There's a lot of BS about. (We'll run through some specific questions to ask about qualifications shortly.)

How To Hire

There are several routes you can take to find a therapist or coach. The most common are:

- A referral from a family doctor or GP
- Word of mouth recommendation
- Through a directory via an eating disorder advice service
- Or through your own online research and social media

No matter how you end up finding a coach or therapist, the questions you should ask to vet them are the same — even if you were referred by a doctor. Never assume someone is going to be right for you; always verify and ask critical questions. Having said this, **certain routes are going to be riskier than others**. Ideally, if you are hiring someone privately, your starting point should be a recognised eating disorder advice service or charity (such as BEAT in the UK or NEDA in the US), which will have a directory of therapists and coaches who specialise in binge eating.

This process isn't foolproof, of course, but it massively increases your chances of finding someone who is credible and qualified as opposed to some random person on the internet. If that's not an option — either because you can't find someone suitable or because your country doesn't have a directory like this — you can still find some great coaches using your own research. Just make sure your BS filter is set super high and you ask tough questions before you hand over any money.

Questions To Ask

- **Do they offer the services you want?** Most binge eating coaches and therapists fall into one of two camps. They are either mental health professionals (such as clinical psychologists) with a specialism in eating disorders, or their background is primarily in diet and nutrition but with added expertise in dealing with disordered eating. Those two camps use different techniques and approaches, so it's useful to know from the start what services someone can offer. If you want advice on food plans and nutrition, someone food-focused (like a registered nutritionist) is going to be a better fit for you than a clinical psychologist.

  Conversely, if cognitive behavioural therapy is what you're after you'll need a mental health professional rather than a dietitian. At the same time, bear in mind that not every mental health professional will offer CBT, so always check before you commit to a session. If you don't yet know what services you might want, speak to your doctor or an advisor at an eating disorder charity, and ask for recommendations.

- **What are their qualifications?** We've already discussed how confusing job titles for therapists and coaches can be, and why it's important for you to do thorough research before hiring someone. So here are some questions to help you determine how qualified someone is:

  - **What's the exact name of their qualification?** You'll find lots of colourful marketing copy floating around coaches' websites (things like 'body positivity evangelist' or 'food empowerment facilitator') that tell you sweet FA. You need to see the actual name of the degree, course, certificate etc. they hold.

o **How hard is it to find out about their qualifications?** There's more than a passing correlation between how well qualified someone is, and how freely they share information about their qualifications. If it takes major investigative effort to find out what qualifications someone holds, ask yourself why.

o **How long did they have to study for their qualification?** Run a search on the name of the qualification that's listed and look at course information for prospective students. Does it take several years of studying? A few months? Are there entry requirements? What about final exams and assessments?

o **Was there a practical component to their qualification?** Again, you'll find this by looking up course information for prospective students. Are there clinical placements and real work with clients involved? Or is it all theory and self-study?

o **Who are they accredited by or registered with?** Most credible therapists and coaches maintain an affiliation with a professional body, not least so they can differentiate themselves from less qualified practitioners. This information should be easily available to you.

o **Has there been any controversy around the qualification they hold?** A simple online search will give you the information you need. Just type in the name of the qualification or professional body, plus 'scandal' or 'controversy', to see if there has been any negative media coverage or concerns raised about standards.

Remember, the goal here is not to discount someone because they don't have a high-calibre qualification. The goal is for you to understand what you're about to spend your time and money on. As an informed consumer, it's your right to know if your coach or therapist had to study five years at university or if they did a six-week correspondence course.

- **How much relevant experience do they have?** Note the emphasis on 'relevant'. You don't want to be someone's first binge eating client, even if they have great qualifications otherwise. In my experience, this is where coaches with slightly lower-grade qualifications can tip the balance back in their favour. Having lots of practical, hands-on experience with binge eaters makes a big difference. However, finding out how much experience someone has can be quite tricky. You can ask outright, of course, but you may not necessarily get an answer that tells you much. Instead, I have found it useful is to ask about experience in a slightly roundabout way:

  - *What first got you interested in working with binge eating clients?*
  - *How does your approach differ when you are dealing with binge eaters as opposed to people with other eating disorders?*
  - *What is the most common recovery mistake you see binge eaters make?*

Then listen out for the level of detail in their answers. Does what they say sound plausible? Do they give examples of clients they've worked with and do those examples sound lifelike? Or are you getting short, one-dimensional answers that provide little insight? It's not a perfect system, but it will help you get some sense of how much exposure to binge eating a coach or therapist may have had. Plus, it should give you greater insight into the particular approach they're taking.

- **What's the structure and what costs can you expect?** A prospective coach or therapist should be able to explain to you how they are going to structure not just individual sessions but your wider recovery process, what the main milestones are going to be, and what time frame they will be working towards. If you are the one footing the bill, you should also be asking for a detailed breakdown of costs before you commit to anything.

That last point is key as you and your therapist need to be on the same page about what you are willing and able to commit to. If you can only afford a few one-off sessions as opposed to months of therapy, you need to make that clear from the start, so the sessions can be structured accordingly. Don't allow anyone to bully you into signing up for more sessions than you can afford. You're the one setting the parameters for your therapist, not the other way around (though your therapist may rightly point out that your results will vary depending on what you can commit to).

If you are hiring an online coach or therapist, asking detailed questions about how sessions are run is especially important as this can vary widely. Will you do the sessions over Skype, for example? Is everything done one-on-one or is there an element of group therapy, such as through a private Facebook group? Can you opt out of that if you're not comfortable with groups, without missing out on crucial information and support? You also want to be absolutely clear on how personalised the sessions are going to be. Are you going to get actual live therapy sessions with a coach every time, just as you would if you were seeing someone in person — or will you be sent video tutorials and instructions via email? There is no right or wrong answer here. Just make sure you know what you're getting.

- **Can you take a trial session?** Some coaches and therapists offer initial consultations or the first session for free; in most cases, however, you should expect to pay for someone's time. What's important is that you should be given the opportunity to get a taste of what therapy sessions or coaching will look like before committing lots of time and money. I would be very cautious about anyone who requires you to sign up for an entire programme in one go, especially if you have to commit money up-front. Therapy and coaching is highly personal and there is no telling in advance whether you are going to work well with a certain coach or therapist.

- **How do they handle failure?** No recovery programme has a perfect success rate. No therapist, no matter how good, will be able to help everyone they encounter. So, what is their attitude when things don't work out? A useful way to establish this is to ask: What percentage of people you work with don't get better? And what is the most common reason why?

  I have found this to be a revealing question for two reasons. First, a therapist who claims a zero percent failure rate is obviously not credible. And if they bristle at the question, that's another red flag. Serious professionals simply won't have a problem admitting what they do doesn't work for everybody. Second, it tends to flush out a nasty streak that some coaches and therapists are guilty of: Blaming the client for a lack of success. This is a favourite trick of the diet industry, where failure is always the dieter's fault and never the programme's. *If you can't stick to a 1,200 calorie-a-day gluten and dairy-free diet, you clearly don't want it enough.* You don't want that kind of attitude in a therapist, so be wary of any insinuation that clients who don't succeed lack commitment, don't work hard enough or don't buy enough sessions to see results. In my experience, it's a clear sign that a coach or therapist lacks accountability.

You might look at this list of questions and wonder if a coach or therapist might take exception to being quizzed like this. Please don't worry about that. Remember it's your money, your time and your health that are at stake here. You absolutely have the right to ask these questions. And again, I can't stress enough: **Serious professionals won't mind.** They will get why you're asking these questions and be happy to answer them to help you make the right decision.

Getting The Most Out Of Working With A Therapist Or Coach

You've done your research and found someone you trust and are comfortable with. Now the real work begins. What your sessions will look like will obviously differ based on what kind of coach you've hired, and whether you're seeing them in person or remotely. But no matter what therapy or coaching you have opted for, there are five core principles that are worth bearing in mind.

- **Don't expect miracles.** I've said this several times already, but it remains true: If you are expecting miraculous, overnight results, you are going to be disappointed. A good therapist or coach can help you make serious progress, but you have to be realistic about the time frames involved. Don't become disheartened if you don't see instantaneous results.

- **Be open-minded.** You have to be willing to try out new things. Recovery is ultimately about change and doing things differently. If your therapist or coach suggests something that takes you out of your comfort zone, don't dismiss it out of hand. Don't assume you know better. Instead, do your best to implement the advice you're given, but let your therapist know if you're struggling and ask for extra support or guidance, if necessary.

- **Be honest.** Your therapist or coach can only help you based on the information you give them. If you lie about your binges, don't tell them about concerns you have or submit fake food diaries, the whole process is pointless. Honesty and transparency are a must. If you are struggling, say so. If you don't like something, say so. If you feel tempted to fake food journals, say so. Give your therapist or coach a chance to help you.

- **Don't run another programme behind their back.** I've done this at times, and it's just the biggest waste of time for everyone involved. If you are in the lucky position of working with a therapist or coach — someone able to give advice and support tailored specifically to you — don't undermine them by secretly following someone else's programme. Don't try out self-help books at the same time, or run food plans and diets, without telling your therapist or coach first. You risk following completely contradictory advice and not getting any results. Focus on one thing at a time.

- **Keep a detailed recovery record.** Chances are your therapist or coach will ask you to do some form of journaling to help with your binge eating, but I'd recommend you also keep brief notes on your sessions. What did you talk about and what advice or exercises were you given? Did the session raise any questions for you? Was there anything you were unsure about? Notes like this will make it easier for you to absorb what you learned, and help you identify potential points of tension or conflict that you may want to discuss in your next session.

What To Do If Things Aren't Working Out

Sometimes, despite your best research and screening efforts, you still end up with a therapist or coach who just isn't right for you. When this happens, it's important that you act quickly and decisively. You need to:

- **Diagnose the problem.** The most important fact you need to establish is whether the therapist/coach is the problem — or the particular type of therapy/coaching you have opted for. Ask yourself:

  o Can you pinpoint a specific moment, exchange or exercise that's made you feel unhappy or uncomfortable? Try to describe it in as much detail as possible.
  o Do you like your therapist/coach?
  o Do you feel you have a genuine connection?
  o What do you imagine would be different if you went to a different therapist/coach?
  o If you feel you want to try out a different therapy style, what do you think it will give you that you're not getting currently? Have you done any research?

- **Sense-check your diagnosis.** Once you've decided whether the therapist/coach is the problem or the therapy/coaching style, run some due diligence on your conclusion. Ask yourself:

  o Have you given your therapist/coach a fair chance?
  o Have you talked to them about your concerns?
  o Have you done what they have told you, or have you altered the programme in some way?
  o Are you feeling disheartened because of a binge?

Remember, a therapist/coach isn't a miracle worker. You will still experience setbacks and binges as you start out on this journey, so it's important you don't throw in the towel as soon as you binge.

- **Take action.** Your first step should be to talk to your therapist or coach. In many cases, they will be able to adjust the sessions or the focus of your programme to address your concerns. Therapists and coaches are professionals, and they will want to do a good job for you. They won't be offended by a bit of feedback. Clearly explain what you're unhappy with and ask what can be done to address the situation. Try to be as specific as possible when describing what you think isn't working, but avoid getting personal or making accusations.

  A good example might be: *'I've been meaning to talk to you about my food diary. I get very stressed about having to keep a constant food log, and I worry it's contributing to my binging. Is there a way we can progress without it?'*

  If the problem is down to a personal clash and you simply want to move on to someone else, the best approach is **politeness and brevity.** You could say something like: *'I don't think this is working for me, so I am going to be taking a break from sessions for now.'* If you are asked questions, only answer as much as you are comfortable. You are under no obligation to explain yourself. Keep things polite, then move on.

TRACKING & JOURNALING

Most recovery programmes require you to do some form of tracking or journaling. Whether it's keeping a log of your eating habits or capturing thought patterns and emotions, you are likely to have to run one, or several, trackers and journals during your recovery process. As tracking and journaling feature in so many recovery methods — self-help or otherwise — it's important you **know how to track and journal effectively.** Trackers and journals are powerful recovery tools, but they can also be very time-consuming — and, if you get it wrong, possibly even counter-productive to your recovery. It's therefore a good idea to be clear from the outset on how tracking and journaling are meant to help you, and what pitfalls to look out for. In this chapter, we'll cover:

- The role of tracking & journaling in recovery
- Why paper is better than digital
- Recovery tracker ideas for you to try
- What not to track
- Bullet journaling for binge eating recovery
- And other styles of journaling

The Role Of Tracking & Journaling In Recovery

Tracking and journaling help you become aware of patterns in your thought processes, emotions and behaviours you may not notice otherwise. This is why they are such an important component of behaviour-based recovery methods such as cognitive behavioural therapy, though many other recovery approaches also make extensive use of journaling and tracking. By writing down what you are doing and feeling at a given moment, you are creating a record you can later review and analyse, either on your own or with a coach or therapist. This is incredibly important, as you are unlikely to develop a deeper understanding of your binge patterns and eating behaviours just by thinking about them. Seeing the facts written down often creates clarity that wasn't there before.

At the same time, the act of tracking and journaling itself can have a positive impact on your behaviour. Spending time to capture your emotions (no matter how briefly) and review your progress can make you less impulsive and more considered.

Tracking vs Journaling

Tracking is primarily concerned with **capturing data** around a specific set of pre-defined behaviours that are important to your recovery. Trackers answer questions such as: Did you binge today? How many times have you meditated in the past week? How much money did you spend on food this month? There's no need to write hundreds of words; often a simple tick or yes/no will do.

Journaling, on the other hand, tends to revolve around **more open-ended questions** and therefore requires more extensive writing. It answers questions such as: How are you feeling today? What are your hopes and fears? How do you believe your recovery is going? Why do you think you ended up binging yesterday?

Of course, it's not always this clear-cut. Some trackers have journaling components (for example, a 'how do you feel' section alongside a food tracker), while many people include data trackers in their journals as well as longer think pieces. In general, however, journaling is focused more on helping you to **discover** behaviours and thoughts patterns that are helpful or harmful to you, while tracking is more about **logging and quantifying** behaviours you have already identified.

Why Paper Is Best

I highly recommend you use pen and paper to track your progress, as opposed to apps or a digital or online journal. There is something very powerful about the physical act of writing by hand, and many respected binge eating recovery programmes (particularly CBT-based ones) make a point of recommending handwriting. I have certainly found writing in a physical journal helps me tap into a different part of my brain and forces me to pay closer attention to what it is I am tracking or writing. It is far too easy to update a habit tracking app with a few mindless taps and without much reflection.

Using a paper-based system also **stops you from constantly checking** your tracker or spending too much time pouring over your recovery journal. Remember, as binge eaters we have a tendency to overthink food and our eating habits, and tracking apps and online journals that are easily available on our phones can fuel this tendency. Before you know it, you've installed fifteen different apps and are spending hours fiddling around with the settings and reviewing progress charts and habit chains. Having a simple paper-based journal at home keeps you focused on the task at hand: To track your progress, reflect on what is and isn't working, and keep a record of your achievements.

There are also **data protection and privacy** concerns to consider. Although the risk is small, it is possible that data from your apps and online journal could be hacked and become public. You simply won't face that same risk with paper.

Choosing A Journal

The type of journal you use is entirely up to you. Go with whatever feels right. My only recommendation is that you pick **only one journal** and try to stick with it throughout your recovery process. I recommend this because some binge eaters have a tendency to start journal after journal, get a few pages in and then throw it away the minute they suffer a setback or have a binge, and start a new one again. It's as if they cannot bear the thought of having 'messed up' their journal. They crave the blank page and the feeling of starting afresh.

I've certainly been guilty of this, and I've had to work hard to fight this impulse. But fight it you must. If you keep abandoning your journal the moment something doesn't go to plan, you will never get the insight that's needed to make real progress. That's why it's so important to commit to only one journal and keep writing in it, no matter what happens. (Obviously, if you run out of space, buy a new one.)

If you are on a recovery programme that requires you to track your food habits throughout the day — and you don't want to carry a notebook with you all the time — I recommend you create log sheets that you can fold up and put in your purse. Simply fill them in during the day and file them away in a ring binder or put them in an envelope at home at the end of the day.

Working With Trackers

Many recovery programmes require you to do some form of tracking (such as keeping track of how often you binge) and will have specific suggestions for what you are meant to be logging in your journal. However, if you are working with a programme that either doesn't require tracking or doesn't have specific suggestions for what you're supposed to keep track of, then I have some ideas for you to try out. Equally, if you are simply keen to try out different tracking styles to see if they might help your recovery, read on.

As always, bear in mind that starting a particular style of tracking doesn't mean you'll have to continue with it forever. Give it a decent amount of time (I'd say at least thirty days) and then move on to something else. There are so many tracking styles out there there's no point spending time on something that's not working for you.

Set Clear Boundaries

The most important lesson I learned over twenty years of binge eating and numerous recovery attempts — as well as numerous journals and trackers — is that your recovery journal and trackers need to be about more than food. **Recovery from binge eating is much more than an absence of binges.** It requires change across different mental, physical and emotional aspects of your life, and your journaling and tracking need to reflect this. If all you ever do is track how much you've binged, write down what you've eaten and spend hours free-writing about your relationship with food, you are only addressing part of the problem.

In fact, my experience tells me spending lots of time logging, tracking and writing about food is not healthy for binge eaters who are already struggling with obsessive thoughts around food and eating. That's why you need to set some boundaries.

Later in this book, we'll talk in detail about how to create goals around non-food behaviours to make sure you're not narrowly obsessing about your food habits. For the time being, my recommendation is this: If you want to track your food habits and binges in some form, limit yourself to tracking only two food-related behaviours at a time. Don't set up countless trackers keeping score of every minor aspect of what you eat.

Ideas For Tracking Your Progress

As I just mentioned, we'll talk about how to set up non-food goals and trackers later. For now, here are some ideas to get you started with tracking your food-related recovery progress. As you'll see, there are advantages and disadvantages to each tracking style — and not all of them might be suitable for you right now. Make sure you are honest with yourself about what kinds of trackers are likely to be helpful to you — and which ones might affect you negatively. Some of the blunter binge trackers (such as counting the number of your binges) can be triggering for some people. If in doubt, steer clear.

- **Tracking your binges**

  How does it work? As the name suggests, you count how often you binge. This can be done with a simple tracker or checklist in your recovery journal. Over time, you will be able to see if you are binging more or less on average as well as any patterns around specific days or times of the month.

  Pros: Straightforward and easy to do. Gives you clear, unambiguous data on your binge frequency.

  Cons: Very negative. Focused solely on something going wrong. Tracking process itself can be upsetting and potentially triggering. Not recommended in the early stages of recovery or if you know you struggle to move on after a binge or get very emotional.

- **Tracking binge-free days**

  How does it work? Instead of tracking when you binge, you keep track of how often you manage not to binge, typically by filling out a tracker in your journal at the end of the day. If you are not at a stage where you have entire binge-free days, this marker can be adapted to track binge-free mornings, evenings, weekends or similar.

  Pros: Focuses on a positive achievement, while still giving you clear data and being easy and straightforward. Could be used together with rewards you create for yourself to help motivate you.

Cons: Not suitable if you have a tendency to think in terms of 'good' and 'bad' days, as a binge early on in the day might encourage you to 'write off' the whole day and binge even more.

- **Tracking your binge spend**

  How does it work? Every time you spend money on binge food, you log it in your journal or an app on your smartphone. (This is one time where phone-based tracking beats paper.) You then review your total spend once a month. This allows you to see just how much money your binges are costing as well as giving you an indication of whether you are spending more or less over time.

  Pros: Minimises triggering by allowing you to keep a tab on your binging without having to focus on the actual binges themselves. Ability to track retrospectively by looking at your bank statement means data accuracy isn't dependent on whether you've managed to track in the heat of the moment. Seeing how much you spend on binges can be highly motivating.

  Cons: Only captures food bought specifically for binging purposes. It can be time-consuming (if not impossible) to separate out food that was bought in general from food that you ended up binging on.

- **Tracking your total food spend**

  How does it work? This is a variation of the binge spend tracker, but instead of tracking food you bought specifically to binge on you track all your food expenses for the month — including your normal family grocery shop, going out for a meal or having a coffee with a friend. You can do this in whichever form you like, using either your journal or an app.

  Pros: Easy to do. No need to figure out retrospectively whether something you bought ended up in a binge or was part of your normal food expenses. Can be a useful early alarm system if you have a tendency to overeat and over-snack in the run up to a binge — if your food spend starts going up, you know to be on the alert. As with the binge spend tracker, seeing how much of your disposable income goes on food can be very motivating in and of itself.

Cons: Data isn't very accurate and can easily be distorted (e.g. if you go out for a fancy restaurant meal one month or deliberately buy super-cheap foods to binge on).

What Not To Track

Unless specifically advised by a credible self-help book or a therapist you're working with, I'd recommend you stay clear of the following:

- Counting calories
- Tracking macros
- Using any kind of food tracking app (e.g. MyFitnessPal)
- Tracking bad or forbidden foods
- Keeping a detailed food diary

Remember, it's very easy for binge eaters to overthink their food choices and spend vast amounts of their day agonising over what they have eaten. Do not play into this by constantly tracking and reviewing what you have eaten.

Bullet Journaling for Binge Eating Recovery

One of the best-known journaling styles around is bullet journaling. The original bullet journal method was developed by an American designer called Ryder Carroll, who wanted an analogue planning tool in a digital world. One of its key components is something called 'rapid logging' — a quick and simple process of capturing, categorising and organising things in your journal using symbols like arrows and circles.

Bullet journals also tend to feature daily, weekly, monthly and yearly overviews or spreads of key tasks and important events.

The benefits of bullet journaling in the context of binge eating recovery are:

- It's a very flexible format that can be customised to your needs
- It can accommodate everything from daily diary entries and morning pages to specific logs and trackers
- The journaling process can be fun and creative, which may help some people stay motivated
- The mix of daily, weekly and monthly spreads helps to keep you focused on longer-term goals
- There is lots of inspiration available online

One of the distinguishing features of bullet journals is that they involve using a blank notebook and creating spreads and pages within it **exactly to your specifications and needs**, as opposed to using a premade diary or journal with sections and prompts that have already been defined. They also tend to have an index at the front and numbered pages, so you can quickly navigate between different sections you have set up. This means it would be very simple to use the trackers, review sheets and journaling styles described in this book all in the same bullet journal, despite how different they all look. Given how important I think it is to stick with one journal for your recovery, this alone means bullet journaling is **my preferred journaling method** for binge recovery.

However, not all bullet journals are focused on functionality. What's arguably propelled bullet journals to stardom is the way you can get creative and make them look amazing. Just search for 'bullet journal' on Instagram, Pinterest or YouTube, and you will find thousands of images and videos of people creating incredibly beautiful spreads, full of colourful charts and trackers. I have no idea whether these journals actually help anyone get their life together, but they are certainly very pretty to look at. However, they are also nothing like the original bullet journal style Carroll developed, which is very minimalistic. Think simple black biro and a few tick boxes as opposed to pages full of intricate calligraphy and washi tape.

This is an important point to keep in mind if you're interested in trying out bullet journaling. Don't be intimidated by how beautiful some people's bullet journals are. It says nothing about their efficacy. If you enjoy being creative and the idea of a nice-looking journal that you can customise appeals to you, by all means go for it, but it's not a requirement. Understand that most of the bullet journals you see online and on social media are quite far removed from the original idea. I would therefore suggest you search out Carroll's website for his take before looking at other people's interpretations.

Other Journaling Styles

- **Morning pages:** Taken from Julia Cameron's self-help classic The Artist's Way, morning pages is a daily writing ritual that involves handwriting three pages in your journal every morning, after you wake up. What you write shouldn't be about anything in particular, just whatever is running through your mind at that moment. Importantly, don't read back as you're writing or try to rephrase or edit sections. Fans of morning pages (including Tim Ferriss) say this helps them clear their mind, connect with their emotions and sets them up for a more productive day.

- **Gratitude journal:** This is a practice where you reflect specifically on the things in your life you are grateful for. A typical prompt might be 'Write down five things from the past week you are grateful for', though there are many different variations and you can find lots of ideas and templates for gratitude journals and writing exercises online. Some people keep a daily gratitude journal, though research suggests weekly journaling could be more effective — possibly because it's less of a struggle to think of new things all the time.

- **Daily log:** As the name suggests, this style of journaling involves committing to writing in your journal every day. You can keep your entries general and about your day-to-day life, or you could keep a daily log focused specifically on anything to do with your binge eating recovery. Daily logging can be a great way to keep you focused on achieving a particular goal, and it doesn't have to be something you do all year round. If you're new to the practice, try setting yourself a thirty-day challenge in the first instance.

- **One line a day:** A variation on daily logging, this method makes the prospect of journaling every day less intimidating because you limit yourself to one line. Thanks to this limitation, some people find their entries end up being more considered and focused than if they had an open-ended word count.

- **Adjective journal:** This is a technique suggested by several journaling-focused self-help books, and it goes like this: Every evening, you write down one adjective that describes how your day has been — and then a second adjective to describe how you'd like the next day to be. As with 'one line a day', this system can make journaling less intimidating and time-consuming, while at the same time encouraging you to really think about which one word best sums up your experience

PART TWO:

THE FIVE PILLARS OF BINGE EATING RECOVERY

PILLAR ONE: SELF-KNOWLEDGE

By now, you've probably noticed that I believe knowledge plays a very important role in recovery. It's why so much of the first part of this book is about building up your knowledge and understanding of binge eating as a mental health condition. I truly believe that knowing the basics about the condition you are trying to fight will stop you from falling for scams and harmful advice; it will empower you to ask for the help you need; and it will help you understand that you are not the only one dealing with this.

However, in addition to understanding the causes, symptoms and treatment options for binge eating, there is another kind of knowledge you will need to master: **Knowledge of yourself as a binge eater.** Forget for a moment about what 'binge eaters' tend to do and how they 'typically' behave. Forget about the stats that tell you X% do this and Y% do that. What are *you* like? What are the unique patterns and behaviours that make up *your* binge eating problem?

You may feel like you have this one covered already. You are, after all, the one who has to deal with your binge eating 24/7. Of course, you know what you're like as a binge eater. But do you really? If I asked you to describe what your binge eating looks like, could you tell me which days of the week and times of day most of your binges take place? Could you give me typical scenarios and locations? Could you identify common emotional triggers? Or would your response be closer to: *'Anywhere and anytime, there's no pattern, it just comes over me and then I can't stop myself?'*

If it's the latter, you don't know nearly enough — and that needs to change. Detailed knowledge of your binge patterns and emotions is crucial for recovery. It enables you to ask for better, more targeted help, and it makes it easier to develop coping strategies and prevention tactics for your binges. Because, at the end of the day, **strategy demands specificity**. You can't begin to formulate coping mechanisms and prevention tactics based on some generic idea of a binge eater. You need something based specifically on you.

So, in this chapter, you will learn:

- How to become **an expert** in your own binge eating
- How to use self-reflection and brainstorming techniques to gain **a new perspective** on your binge patterns and behaviours
- How to use that knowledge to develop **prevention tactics** for your binges

Becoming Your Own Binge Eating Expert

We are going to use **six worksheets** to help you become an expert in your own binge eating. You can find these at the back of the book, where you will also find detailed instructions for how to complete them. Before you jump into doing the exercises, however, I recommend you finish reading this chapter so you understand exactly how they are meant to be used.

The first important point you need to know is that you can get free, printable versions of all worksheets in this book at www.bingeeatingrecoveryproject.com/worksheets

The second key point is that the worksheets are not diagnostic tools. You won't get a score at the end to tell you how 'good' or 'bad' a binge eater you are, or what you should do next based on your answers. They are meant to help with self-awareness and self-reflection only. The value of doing the exercises lies purely in taking some time to think about your binge eating and explore your emotions around it.

Nor are the exercises based on some unique insight into binge eating psychology. After all, I'm not a mental health professional. They are simply a collection of useful questions and prompts I have encountered or developed over the years. Indeed, lots of them are fairly standard stuff that you'll see in many self-help books or when working with therapists or coaches.

The main difference is the format. I wanted to make the process of reflection more manageable and less intimidating. So many self-help books I read over the years—and even some therapists I worked with — told me it was important that I reflect on my binge eating. Yet I could never work out what that meant in practice. I was always left wondering: What are you supposed to reflect on? Are you meant to sit down and just *think*? This is why you will see lots of multiple-choice questions on my worksheets. My experience has taught me that instead of trying to answer open-ended questions like *'Why do you think you binge?'*, it's often easier to recognise thought patterns and underlying attitudes in yourself when someone else spells them out for you. All you have to do, then, is decide whether you agree or disagree.

Doing these worksheets and exercises might also help you talk about your binge eating to other people. You may even decide to share some of your completed worksheets with a therapist or coach.

A Different Way To Track

Another reason I have found worksheets and questionnaires so useful in my own recovery is because I was always terrible at tracking and logging my binges. That turned out to be a bit of a problem, as lots of self-help programmes and therapy methods rely on you keeping a log or a journal. You are meant to write down when you binge, what time of day it was, how you were feeling at the time, as well as any triggers, in the hope that, over time, this will help you become more aware of your binge eating patterns.

Unfortunately, this process doesn't work for everyone. Although other forms of tracking and journaling have been very useful to me, including many of those described in the previous chapter, I often found that the very act of tracking meant I was not behaving as I normally would. Suddenly I would be on my best behaviour, logging binge-free day after binge-free day until the inevitable happened — at which point I simply stopped logging altogether and vowed to start again from scratch. As a result, my logs and journal entries were **completely inauthentic**. They did not in any way capture what I really did as a binge eater. I had to find another way.

The best way I found is retrospective study. Instead of trying to capture what you are doing in real time, you look back at your binges and try to identify patterns by asking questions in a structured way. The questions on the worksheets are what I used to create that structure.

Of course, if you are someone who is able to keep authentic real-time logs of your binges, then there is absolutely no reason for you to stop doing what you're doing. By all means use the worksheets as well, but don't feel compelled to change something that's working for you.

What To Expect From The Worksheets

- **Your Binge Profile:** The main purpose of this worksheet is to collect metrics to help quantify and describe your binge eating. You will be answering detailed questions about how often you binge as well as when and where, using a mixture of multiple choice, yes/no and open-ended question formats.

- **Finding Your Archetypal Binge:** This is all about being able to describe — clearly and precisely — the key characteristics and scenarios that encapsulate your binge eating problem in its most common form. I'm calling this your archetypal binge. It's your binge eating behaviour in a nutshell. If someone asked me to describe a typical 'Jen Lessel' binge, I would give them a description of my archetypal binge. (You can read that very description later.)

- **Reverse-Engineering A Good Day:** What goes right when you have a good day? And how can you create those circumstances more often? This worksheet is going to help you answer those questions, while encouraging you to take a positive, constructive approach towards managing your binges.

- **Binge Questionnaire:** The questionnaire will lead you to explore your attitudes and emotions towards your binge eating problem — especially emotions you may not want to admit to yourself. You will be presented with a list of statements about binge eating and be asked to indicate how much you agree or disagree with them on a scale of 1 to 5.

- **Understanding Your Triggers:** As the name suggests, you will be asked questions around your binge eating triggers to help improve your awareness and understanding of how triggers affect your eating patterns. The format is primarily yes/no and multiple choice, with some open-ended questions.

- **Finish The Sentence:** An alternative to the multiple choice and yes/no format, this particular worksheet calls on you to express your emotions around your binge eating. You will be shown a list of half-finished sentences about binge eating, which you will need to complete in your own words.

Using Self-Knowledge To Develop Prevention Tactics

Unlike many self-help books and articles you find online, I am not going to give you prevention tips to try. I don't have a list of *'25 things to do instead of binging'* or *'40 ways to prevent a binge'*. That's because, in my experience, these sorts of lists tend to be close to useless. The problem is that the suggestions are either too generic or super-specific to one person (usually the author of the article). Neither is going to be of much help to you.

I believe the best coping and prevention strategies respond directly and specifically to your circumstances, patterns and behaviours as a binge eater. They don't generically tell you to be more mindful, drink a glass of water, count to three or take a relaxing bath, because those things may not be viable when you're about to binge. You need something that's custom-made for you. To be able to create something custom-made, you need to know your binge patterns and behaviours inside out. And you need a crystal-clear idea of what **your most common binge scenario** is. The Archetypal Binge worksheet will help you with that. If you haven't completed it yet, now's a good time to do so. Before we go further, I also want to stress two important points:

1) **We'll focus on tactics, not strategies.** This may seem like a pedantic semantic quibble, but they are not the same. The key difference is that strategy is focused on long-term results, while tactics are used to achieve a specific outcome in the short term. Applied to our context, you could say that strategy is about your overall recovery from binge eating, while tactics are about preventing an individual binge. One cannot replace the other. If all you ever do is employ short-term prevention tactics and don't work on your wider mental health, body image or attitude towards food, your recovery efforts are likely to fail. Conversely, if you are only thinking in big picture terms, you are likely to

overlook simple, pragmatic steps you can take to drastically reduce your binges.

2) **You won't be able to prevent every binge.** Sometimes the urge will be too strong; sometimes you might not be in the right frame of mind to say no. With a bit of practice and the right tactics, however, I firmly believe you will be able to do something about the *majority* of your binges.

My Archetypal Binge

Throughout this chapter, I am going to be using my own personal Archetypal Binge as a reference to help illustrate my points. It's based on what my binging was like a few years ago, and goes as follows: *It's a weekday evening, most likely a Wednesday or Thursday. I'm on the train home from work. As I get to my train station and get off the train, I don't go straight home but instead take a detour and stop off at the shops. I tell myself I will only buy a small, healthy snack but then I pick up more and more as I walk around the shop until I reach that dreaded 'might as well' point and go all in. I then eat what I have bought immediately and rapidly, while walking home, and often continue binging once I get home.*

As you can see, I am able to name:

- Specific locations
- Specific days and times of day
- A specific scenario

This is important as developing successful prevention tactics is all about being as specific as possible. I cannot stress this enough. Of course, not all of my binges looked like my Archetypal Binge, but lots of them did — and that meant I could prioritise. You don't have endless time and energy at your disposal, so try to get the most bang for your recovery buck by dealing with your most common binge scenario first.

Finding The Right Tactics

In many ways, simply being more knowledgeable about your binge eating will open your eyes to possible binge prevention tactics. Once I understood that my Archetypal Binge was after work, at the train station, I felt much more optimistic about being able to prevent binges. Suddenly, I was no longer facing a big, intimidating question such as *'How do I stop binging?'* but something much more specific: *'On Wednesdays and Thursdays, how do I get out of the station and home without binging?'* To answer that question, I used three techniques:

- **Brainstorming:** Using creative and lateral thinking to come up with prevention ideas
- **Positive cues:** Using a mantra or mental prompt to keep focused during binge situations
- And **reverse-engineering:** Using retrospection to determine what goes right on a good day and figuring out ways to make that happen more often

Brainstorming

Brainstorming is a great starting point for getting you to think creatively about binge prevention tactics and explore options you wouldn't think of normally. The initial goal is to come up with as many ideas as possible for how to prevent binges. Don't worry about the quality of the ideas at this stage; we'll deal with that later. Crucially, the ideas must be **directly related** to your Archetypal Binge situation. This means they must reflect:

- Where you are at the time of the Archetypal Binge

- What day and time it is
- Which objects you are likely to have on you (e.g. a phone)

Ask yourself: What could you do in that very moment, in that very location, at that very time of day, that might make a difference? Try to come up with at least ten ideas using any brainstorming technique of your choice. As a starting point, here are five of my favourites:

1) **Freewriting:** Sit down with your journal or notebook and write non-stop for a set amount of time. I recommend starting with ten minutes. During that period, you do not pause for any reason; you write without interruption. If you can't think of any ideas, write *'I cannot think of anything right now'* until something comes into your head.

2) **Rolestorming:** Imagine how another person might approach the same situation and write down the kinds of solutions they would come up with to stop themselves from binging. It can be someone you know personally, or a celebrity or other role model you admire.

3) **Wildest Idea Technique:** Come up with the craziest binge prevention tactic you can think of. You'll have every grocery store blacklist you and kick you out if you try to buy food? Sure, why not. How about getting your jaw wired shut? Or having a swat team descend on your house if you approach the fridge? Nothing is too extreme and nothing is off limits. Let your fantasy run wild.

4) **Random stimulation:** Take any book on your book shelf or e-reader, flip to page 73 and read the fifth sentence on that page. Now try to come up with a binge prevention idea based on that sentence. Random stimulation is all about getting you to think

laterally by giving you unconnected things to think about. The idea isn't that whatever is on page 73 is the actual solution to your problem; it's to give your brain a bit of a jolt in the hope that this will unearth some new ideas you wouldn't have thought of otherwise.

5) **Catastrophising:** This is where you get to indulge in all your worst fears about your ability to stop binging. Write down all the ways you are going to try not to binge — and how you'll fail miserably. Really go into detail here and think through exactly why the solutions you've come up with are awful and will never stop you from binging. The process of allowing yourself to think those things and write them down might make you come up with better solutions than the ones you had originally. At the very least, it's cathartic and gets your fears and self-sabotaging tendencies out of your head and onto paper.

As with all brainstorming, **don't censor yourself** and don't dismiss any ideas as they come to you. Write down everything you can think of. After that, look through your list to see if there are any seeds of a good idea that you want to try out or develop further. Most importantly, don't worry if your first round of brainstorming doesn't result in anything you think is usable. You don't need to get this right at first try. Give it a week and then do the exercise again (perhaps with different brainstorming techniques this time) and see what you come up with.

Creating Positive Cues

I believe firmly in the power of mindset, so in addition to practical prevention tactics I wanted to come up with a mantra or mental prompt that would help me stay focused during my Archetypal Binge situations. This is how I ended up stumbling upon the concept of positive cues, which I have found to be enormously helpful in my recovery.

Somewhat bizarrely, it all started with a weightlifting session at the gym. The type of lifting I was training at the time is very technical, and technique drills take up a lot of time during training sessions, especially if you're a beginner. During one of those sessions I kept missing lifts because I let the barbell swing forward. I knew what I was doing was wrong, I could see the bar path was messed up, and yet I wasn't able to correct it. The harder I tried not to swing, the more the bar swung out.

After multiple missed lifts, my coach stopped me and told me to sit down. *'What's going through your head before you start the lift?'* he asked. I sighed. *'Don't swing the bar,'* I said. *'I know. I don't understand why I keep doing it.'* My coach replied: *'No, that's precisely the problem. You keep thinking about the thing you're not supposed to do instead of focusing on what you should do to get the lift right. Don't tell yourself not to swing; tell yourself to keep the bar close to your body.'* I nailed the lift after that.

We moved on with the session, but what my coach had said stayed with me. Because in that moment I understood that I had made a huge oversight in my prevention tactics to date. I had made them all about avoiding something negative — that is, a binge — instead of actively focusing on doing something positive. After my experience in the gym, I knew this had to change. I had to figure out the binge eating equivalent of 'keep the bar close'.

The White Bear Problem

I started doing some research and found more and more evidence to support what my coach had known instinctively: That action is far easier than avoidance; that positive cues that tell you what to do (*'keep the bar close'*) work much better than negative cues that tell you what not to do (*'don't swing'*).

This is partly to do with a psychological phenomenon known as the White Bear Problem. If I tell you not to think of a white bear, then suddenly that's all you're able to think about. This phenomenon explains why constantly thinking about a behaviour you're trying to avoid is a bad idea. If you keep telling yourself 'don't binge', then what you actually end up doing is thinking about binging all the time.

Instead, you need to find something else — something positive — to focus on, which will steer you away from the behaviour you're trying to avoid. Finding that 'something else', however, requires a bit of work. As I've mentioned before, broad, generic cues like 'eat mindfully' or 'stay in the moment' are of limited use. You want a simple single action that is going to move you away from binging at a specific moment. To illustrate this a bit more, let me talk you through how I developed my positive cues.

Positive Cues in Action

I already knew that my Archetypal Binge happened on Wednesdays and Thursdays, in the evening, after work. This was a useful starting point but not nearly precise enough to start formulating a positive action. I was still stuck thinking 'don't binge after work'. I had to analyse my actions further.

So, I mapped out, step by step, exactly what I did during one of those binge eating episodes after work. As I mentioned before, I would take the train back home, I'd get off at my train station and then, instead of going straight home, I would stop off at the shops. I'd tell myself I would only buy a small, healthy snack but then I would pick up more and more as I walked around the shop until I reached that dreaded 'might as well' point and went all in — especially if work had been stressful that day. I would then eat what I had bought immediately and rapidly, while walking home, and would often continue binging once I got home.

Looking at this sequence of events, it was clear the crucial moment was deciding to go to the shops instead of going home. This was the pattern I had to break. To begin with, therefore, I decided to tell myself 'go home'. This would be my positive cue that I would focus on after work. Over time, however, I found I needed to be even more specific in what I was telling myself to do, so I went back into analysis mode and looked at the exact steps involved in going home versus not going home: Getting off the train, walking up the ramp towards the ticket office, going through the ticket barriers and then turning right to go to the shops — or left to go home.

I chose my positive cue based on that simple insight. If I was turning left at the ticket barriers, I wasn't going to the shops — and I most likely wasn't going to binge. So *'turn left'* is what I tell myself as I get off the train and make my way to the ticket office — even to this day. It's what I tell myself as I go through the barriers. *'Turn left.'* I focus on that one single action: *'Turn left.'* It's not a miracle cure, of course. Some days I still ended up turning right. Some days I turned left and then ended up binging at home. But in the majority of cases, I really did turn left and didn't binge.

Once I experienced how useful positive cues could be, I made a point of developing them for other key binge moments. I now have a positive cue for when I still end up at the shops despite my best efforts (*'buy flowers'*); I have a positive cue for when I get home (*'go take a shower'*); I have a positive cue for when I have bought binge food (*'message my boyfriend'*).

Crucially, none of these cues is difficult to execute. They are all super-simple actions that I can do without any preparation or special effort. I am not telling myself to 'do yoga' or 'meditate' when I am at the station, because that's not a viable choice for me right at that moment. The choice I *do* have is where I go next: Do I turn left or right? So that's what I focus on.

Reverse-Engineering A Good Day

The final technique that helped me to come up with ideas for how to prevent binges is a bit of reverse-engineering. This involves working backwards to identify which factors ultimately led to a positive outcome.

In our case, the positive outcome we want to achieve is, of course, not binging. Because I believe this is such a helpful technique, I have created a **dedicated worksheet** for it, which you can find at the back of this book. There you will also find instructions for how to start using reverse-engineering in your own recovery.

First, however, I want to give you a bit of context for why I think reverse-engineering is so useful. Importantly, it gets you to focus on positive outcomes. As we've seen with positive cues and the White Bear Problem, shifting your focus away from the behaviour you want to avoid and towards positive action you can take instead is very powerful. Secondly, the reverse-engineering exercise encourages you to **look beyond food**. The worksheet will present you with lots of questions about what else is happening in your life when things go right for you.

This is incredibly important as binge eating is more than simply a food management problem, and recovery from binge eating takes more than an absence of binges. As you will see, looking beyond food is going to be a recurring theme throughout this book. The insight you will gain from completing the reverse-engineering worksheet will play a critical role later, when you will be setting goals for your recovery.

OVER TO YOU

1) Complete the following worksheets: Binge Profile, Finding Your Archetypal Binge and Reverse-Engineering A Good Day.

2) Schedule a session for a week's time, when you will complete the other three sheets on self-awareness and self-reflection. (Really do your best to resist the temptation to complete all six worksheets at once.)

3) Set aside half an hour and brainstorm prevention ideas based on your Archetypal Binge. Try to come up with at least ten different ideas, using a variety of brainstorming techniques. Remember not to censor yourself.

4) Come up with at least one positive cue for your Archetypal Binge. Make sure you are being as specific as possible.

PILLAR TWO: TIME

I'm just going to put this bluntly: Recovery is going to take longer than you think. How long exactly I don't know. It's different for everybody. What I *do* know is that many of us tend to underestimate the time frames involved in recovery. This chapter is going to fix that. The next few pages will help you develop a much more realistic sense of how long your recovery is likely to take. It will also give you practical tips and ideas for how to structure that time productively.

The main tool we're going to use is the concept of **the recovery year**. At the end of this chapter, you are going to commit to spending the next twelve months on your recovery. Yes, I said twelve months. Don't worry if that sounds impossible right now. I'll walk you through it step by step. In this chapter, we'll cover:

- Why it's so important to set a **realistic time frame** for recovery
- Why deadlines and time-specific goals aren't a great idea for binge eaters
- **What to do** during your recovery year — and what not to
- And how to make your commitment official and **hold yourself accountable**

Why You Need A Year

In my experience, what dooms recovery attempts more than anything are unrealistic expectations. And nowhere are unrealistic expectations more common than in relation to time frames. This shouldn't come as a surprise. We are surrounded by stories of quick, transformational change. It's what every TV makeover show, from plastic surgery to interior design, is based on. It's what New Year's resolutions are all about. And don't even get me started on diet culture, with its promises of 'Six weeks to your bikini body' and 'Thirty-day clean eating challenges'.

Wherever we look, the message is: Radical change can happen quickly. That's why we assume six weeks or thirty days are reasonable time frames for achieving meaningful change. Let's be clear, they're not. They're eye-catching marketing promises that exploit our desperation and our desire for quick fixes. They distract us from the important foundational work that's needed to build sustainable change, and instead push us towards rash, short-term action that ends up undermining our long-term health and wellbeing. What's more, they gloss over all the boring hard work that needs to happen in between the 'before' and 'after' picture.

Editing out the boring stuff in the middle makes sense if you're putting together a makeover show, but it doesn't work in the real world. **The boring stuff in the middle isn't optional.** It's where most of your recovery takes place. If you want to get good at recovery, you are going to have to get good at the boring stuff in the middle — and that takes time. After all, you didn't develop your binge eating problem overnight. It's unrealistic to expect to undo all the patterns and behaviours you've ingrained during your binge eating years in a few weeks or months.

Before we dive more deeply into the rationale and benefits of a full recovery year, I want to stress one important point: Committing to a year of recovery doesn't mean one year is all it's going to take. You're not setting yourself a deadline, nor are you saying you'll be done once the twelve months are up. Right now, you aren't in a position to predict how long your recovery will take. It could be a year; it could be less; it could be more.

The one-year time frame is simply a device to provide you with the structure and help you need to get away from short-term thinking. It's also a useful reference point to ensure we are on the same page whenever I talk about allowing a decent amount of time for your recovery. Otherwise some people may be tempted to interpret that as meaning six weeks!

Slow Is Fast

Getting good at the boring stuff between the 'before' and 'after' is about making small, incremental changes that, together, add up to dramatic change over time. Creating change in this way is much more sustainable and achievable than making lots of big, radical changes. Although these can yield good results in the short term, **the results rarely last**. Crash diets are the obvious example. Yes, people lose weight quickly, but the diets are so extreme they can't stick to them for more than a short period of time. Once they go off the diet, the weight comes back (and then some) and they're back to square one. This is why attempts at radical change often end up costing you more time than the seemingly slower approach of going for small, consistent progress.

That's not all. If you're always chasing radical change, you will be tempted to do too many things at once. This is likely to hurt your progress. Suddenly you are trying to implement a whole raft of new habits and actions which — while perfectly sensible in their own right — become unmanageable if you're dealing with them all at the same time. You are more likely to succeed if you tackle **one change or habit at a time** and allow it to integrate into your routine before moving on to the next one. Indeed, it's what most behaviour change experts advocate. Leo Babauta's well-respected *Zen Habits* programme, for example, asks people to pick one simple habit and embed it into their everyday routine for a full three months before trying anything more complex.

You're not going to see dramatic overnight transformations with that approach, of course, but habits created this way are more likely to stick long term. You'll also end up with better data and insight on what works for you. If you change everything at once, you don't actually know which bits are working for you — and which are a waste of your time. And remember, incremental progress can still add up to big, transformational change over time. Those small pieces of change are not your final destination — they're stepping stones towards your bigger goal.

Kaizen Or The 1% Rule

One helpful way to think about creating small, incremental progress in your life is the so-called kaizen method, sometimes also known as the 1% rule. Kaizen is Japanese and translates as 'change for better'. It is an influential philosophy of continuous improvement, which is used in personal development as well as a wide range of business and industry, from healthcare to supply chain logistics. The company best known for using kaizen techniques is Japanese car manufacturer Toyota, which managed to boost productivity by encouraging its workers to constantly look for small improvements they can make to their day-to-day work.

For our purposes, the key point is that kaizen is a daily practice which focuses on creating big change through small, manageable steps that can be implemented straight away. The 1% rule (also referred to as the compound interest rule) is one way you can put kaizen principles into action in your everyday life. Every day, week or month you aim to become one percent better than you were before. On their own, those single one percent improvements may seem insignificant. Over time, however, they stack up and compound, and you end up building something truly life- changing.

Kaizen and the 1% rule are particularly useful concepts for binge eating recovery because they emphasise gradual, daily action and move you away from dramatic goals like 'zero binges'. In doing so, they also encourage you to ask deeper questions about your recovery and what you are trying to achieve during your recovery process, including:

- What does gradual improvement look like for you?
- What could you do right now to ensure you are making one percent more progress in your recovery than yesterday?

If you're drawing a blank at these questions or are finding it hard to think of anything other than *'I wouldn't binge'*, don't worry. The process takes a bit of practice. Importantly, don't get caught up in trying to calculate exactly what one percent improvement looks like. This isn't about having you work out a one percent reduction in your binge calorie intake. It's about staying true to the spirit of the idea. That means instead of pursuing dramatic improvements, you go after genuinely **small increments of positive change**.

For example, your improvement could be spending £1 or $1 less on your binges this week. Or it could be having one extra binge-free day this month. Or, if you are binging several times a day, perhaps you could commit to trying to cut one of those instances out on one day in the next fortnight. It doesn't matter how small the improvements are when you're starting out. What matters is that you are moving in the right direction.

Time To Learn

Another important reason for giving yourself a full year for your recovery is that you are in for a steep learning curve. Right now, you are excellent at being a binge eater, but **your skills as a non-binge eater aren't so hot**. No surprises there. After all, you've spent lots of time perfecting your binge eating routine and not nearly as much time practicing not binging. To recover, you are first going to have to learn how not to be a binge eater, and then you are going to have to practice not binge eating until you are good at it.

When you first try out a new self-help programme or begin working with a therapist, you are probably going to suck at it. You might be terrible at tracking your eating, you might fail to complete the exercises your coach asks you to do, and you might even fail to see any reduction at all in your binge eating initially.

Most people become discouraged and quit at this point, thinking the programme isn't working, when it's much more likely that they simply haven't hit their stride yet. They haven't given it enough time to become good at doing the programme, which means they're in no position to decide whether the programme is or isn't working for them. It's important you avoid this trap. **Having a bit of a rough start to a new programme is completely normal.** Don't write off good books or coaches because things don't click straight away. Go into the process knowing you may not be great at this at first, give it a reasonable bit of time and stick with the process before jumping to conclusions.

Crucially, finding the recovery process hard says nothing about your character, motivation or self-discipline. Even super-motivated and committed people can find it tough to deal with the day-to-day reality of recovery. This is nothing to feel bad about. What you're experiencing is a simple skills gap: A gap between what you want to do and what you're currently capable of doing. All you need to close that gap is a bit of time and practice.

There's one more important reason why I recommend you commit to a recovery year: It will **recalibrate your sense of perspective**. If you have twelve months to play with, you are less likely to freak out over a single 'bad' day. After all, you have 365 days with 1,095 meals over the course of a year. Even if you binge every day for a whole month, that's still less than ten percent of the recovery period you're committing to.

Feeling like a small slip-up has ruined everything is one of the biggest reasons people abandon their recovery prematurely. By setting a deliberately long time frame for your recovery, you will avoid this mistake.

If the thought of taking a year to recover still terrifies you, try to remember this: **You will live those twelve months anyway.** The time will pass regardless of whether you choose to do something productive with it. Short-term goals haven't helped you break your binge eating habit so far, so why waste another twelve months doing the exact same thing when you could be using that time to start making some real progress?

Your Recovery Year

Hopefully by now you're on board with the idea of committing to a full year of recovery and are starting to feel excited about what you will be able to achieve over the next twelve months. Here's what's next:

- You need to set goals for your recovery year
- Understand some important dos and don'ts
- Make a formal commitment

Let's start by spending a bit of time thinking about goal setting, and common traps and pitfalls to avoid when setting goals for your recovery year. Lots of self-help literature is based around goals, deadlines and milestones to hold yourself accountable. It usually goes a bit like this: After the first month you want to have achieved X. And after the second month, you want to have done Y. And six months down the line, you are expecting to be at Z.

This is a perfectly sensible approach in lots of areas of life. If you want to run a marathon, become an entrepreneur, supercharge your career or overhaul your personal finances, for example, goals and deadlines will be critical to your success. However, for something like binge eating they can be problematic. This is because outcome-focused goal setting — where you tell yourself you're going to achieve a certain outcome by a certain date — relies on a degree of **linearity and predictability**. Let's take running as an example. If you've managed to get from zero running to doing a 5k in three months, it's fair to assume another three months of training might get you to 10k.

This is not how recovery from binge eating works. Sometimes you see nice, linear progress; at other times it happens in random spurts; sometimes you even end up going backwards for a while. If you were to sit down with a calendar right now and draw up some recovery milestones you want to hit over the next year, **it would be pure guesswork**.

The second reason why goals and deadlines can be tricky is because they play into the kind of **all-or-nothing thinking** many binge eaters struggle with. Goals and deadlines that clearly delineate success from failure are probably a bad idea for someone who's already seeing everything in black and white.

The third reason I want you to be cautious about goal setting is that **it implies that at some point you are going to be 'done'.** You can cross binge eating off your to-do list and never worry about it again. There will be some people for whom this is true, but by no means everybody. In many cases, recovery from binge eating doesn't stop. It is something you need to keep working on during your recovery year and beyond.

Setting Goals

Having said all this, how should you approach goal setting for the next twelve months? I suggest you think of one overarching main goal and several smaller process goals that support your main goal. I also have a suggestion for what your main goal should be: **Not quitting.** For the next twelve months, your most important goal should be not to quit. It's that simple. All of your energy should be focused on making sure that no number of setbacks, binges or lack of progress will derail you. You will promise yourself that you won't lose faith, go 'wild' for a while and then start again from scratch a few weeks or months later. **You will gut this one out no matter what.** There is no being on or off the wagon anymore. If something goes wrong, you dust yourself off, you learn your lessons and you get back to work.

Now, if you're thinking, *'But really my big goal is being binge-free or losing weight or preferably both'*, no problem. Such feelings are normal. It's how I felt too. What's important is that you do not act on those feelings for the next twelve months, because you now understand that pursuing goals of this kind will hurt you.

Creating A Hero Habit

But what does having a big goal like 'not quitting' look like in practice, on a day-to-day basis? What's worked for me is having **one simple habit** that you perform every day. It's what I call a recovery hero habit. It symbolises your commitment to your recovery year and is what you will use to measure whether you are staying true to that commitment. As long as you keep performing your hero habit you have not failed in your recovery attempt, not matter what is happening with your binging or your weight. For this technique to be effective, however, you need to **set the bar deliberately low.** Your hero habit should:

- Be very easy to perform every day
- Not take up lots of time
- Not depend on special equipment
- Not be tied to a specific location
- Not require you to spend money
- Not be in any way related to food or your eating habits

A good example would be committing to making the bed every morning or washing your hair every day or, if you are religious or spiritual, making time for a quick prayer, devotional or meditation every day. In my own case, I've made writing in my journal my hero habit. As long as I write at least one sentence a day, no matter how rushed or uninspired at times, I have done enough to meet my **minimum recovery requirement.**

You might be wondering what happens if you fail to perform your recovery hero habit one day. Game over? Far from it. In addition to setting the bar deliberately low on the type of habit you're going to pick, you'll also give yourself a **deliberately wide margin for error**. I recommend you work with an 80:20 split, calculated over the course of an entire year. What this means in practice is that, out of 365 days, you will have 73 days where you can fail to perform your daily hero habit and still be on track with your overall recovery commitment. Put another way, from the moment you make your recovery year commitment you could theoretically have more than two full months of failing to do your hero habit, and still be on track.

There's an obvious theme here. This is all about making it as hard as possible for you to decide you've failed at your recovery and need to start over. You want to be so generous in your definition of progress that it'll be pretty much impossible for you to fall short. We're doing this because giving up prematurely is one of the biggest risks you are going to face when going through recovery. You need to do everything you can to stack the odds in your favour.

Process Goals

Alongside your hero habit, you should set several process goals that support you in your recovery efforts. Process goals, as the name suggests, are goals that describe what you intend to do, not the outcome you want to achieve. They can be incredibly helpful during recovery because they give you **something concrete to do right now** as opposed to hoping for change at some point in the future. In a nutshell, process goals are:

- Positive
- Action-focused
- Concerned with the day-to-day process of recovery
- Not tied to a deadline or outcome

To find your own process goals, start by asking yourself: *What does a person who is in recovery do?* Don't focus on what they *don't* do (such as binging); focus on the kinds of actions a person who is in recovery would perform. Initially, think specifically of food-related actions and write down as many as you can think of. There is a form you can use later in this book or at www.bingeeatingrecoveryproject.com/worksheets Here are a few examples to get you started:

- A person recovering from binge eating...*eats three meals a day.*
- A person recovering from binge eating...*eats foods from all food groups.*
- A person recovering from binge eating...*makes time to sit down for dinner.*

Next, write down a list of non-food actions a person in recovery would perform. This is important because your binge eating problem is more than just your binges — and recovery from it will take more than an absence of binges. Here are some more examples:

- A person recovering from binge eating...*writes in her journal every day.*
- A person recovering from binge eating...*makes her bed every morning.*
- A person recovering from binge eating...*makes time to read books.*

Now, let's apply the process to you specifically. You'll find this easier if you have already completed the self-reflection exercises featured in the previous chapter, particularly the exercise on reverse-engineering a good day. Ask yourself: **What will you do when you're in recovery** and doing well? What will your day look like? What food-related actions will you perform? And what non-food-related ones? Again, make two lists and write down as many actions as you can. Ideally, you should be aiming for five food and five non-food actions.

As you write down your actions, remember to keep everything **positive**. It's very tempting to come up with endless lists of no-nos and forbidden things. However, you need goals for something you can actually do, not something you need to avoid doing. (See also: The White Bear Problem)

There are some more ideas for you to take inspiration from in the section below. Don't worry if you're not entirely sure about the process goals you're coming up with at this stage. None of this is written in stone. You can always revise your goals as you progress through your recovery year. My only recommendation is that you don't do this on a whim but have some form of review process. Using the Thirty Day Rule described earlier is a good starting point. You don't want to get into the habit of discarding goals too quickly.

Five Ideas For Process Goals

If you are struggling to think of useful process goals for your recovery, take a look at the following sections for some inspiration. My own personal process goals are also listed below, so you can get an idea of what this approach looks like in real life.

- **Personal care & hygiene goals:** Some binge eaters (myself included) struggle to take care of themselves properly when their mental health declines. Suddenly, teeth aren't brushed as regularly, clothes are left un-ironed and hair that's normally styled carefully goes unwashed. Body avoidance often plays a part in this. Keeping track of personal care and hygiene patterns can therefore be an early warning system that lets you know if you are potentially at higher risk of binging. Focusing on positive personal care habits can also be helpful when coming back from a period of binging and body avoidance.

  At various points in my recovery, I have therefore set process goals around applying body lotion after a shower every day; ironing my shirts every Sunday; and doing my nails and applying fresh nail polish once a week. The body lotion goal was particularly helpful in getting me to spot body avoidance tendencies, while the weekly shirt ironing and nail polish routine made me feel prepared and ready for the week ahead. I still use it to this day. No matter what's happening in my life, I always feel a little better with a crisp shirt on and my nails done. *Other ideas for you to consider:* Daily shower, washing your hair, taking a long bath, brushing your teeth, flossing, plucking or shaping your eyebrows, waxing, shaving, polishing your shoes, taking your clothes to be dry cleaned, curling or straightening your hair, applying a hair or face mask, doing your makeup, taking your makeup off before bed, giving yourself a manicure or pedicure, getting a massage

- **Social life & intimacy goals:** Social isolation and loneliness are some of the worst aspects of binge eating. It's all too easy to shut yourself off from others when you are struggling with your eating and feeling uncomfortable in your own skin. You may find socialising overwhelming, get anxious about having to eat in front of others or avoid social contact or intimacy because you don't like the way you look. It's very important you tackle these feelings as part of your recovery. This means spotting and understanding when and how you shut yourself off from others as well as challenging yourself to keep connected to those who care about you. Having recovery goals around your social life and/or your relationships can help you in that effort.

  For example, I tend to start pulling out of social engagements if my binging gets worse and I feel bad about the way I look. This why a dedicated goal to make sure I go out and see a friend at least twice a month has been helpful for me. I don't count social engagements with work colleagues as part of my goal, as I know I am less likely to be concerned about what they think about me.

Other ideas for you to consider: Calling a family member, kissing or having sex with your partner, meeting new people, attending networking events, going to a parents evening, going to church, talking to a neighbour, going to a birthday party, having a birthday party, going on a date, going for after-work drinks, attending a course or lecture.

- **Mental space goals:** Many people with binge eating problems spend an unusual amount of their time thinking about food, diets as well as their body weight and shape. Whether it's meal prepping, weighing yourself, reading about new diets, looking at food pictures on social media or even something as seemingly innocuous as watching cooking shows on TV, thoughts about food can come to dominate your day and, therefore, indirectly contribute to your binge eating problem. This is why finding hobbies and past times that take you away from food is critical. (You'll learn more about the importance of mental space later.) A goal focused on creating mental space away from food will act as a reminder for you to develop new interests and limit the amount of time you spend dwelling on food.

  I know from the reverse-engineering exercise that my wellbeing improves dramatically when I make time every day to read a book, so this is one of my recovery goals. It doesn't have to be long — I usually read for half an hour in the evening — but it makes all the difference. Reading takes me away from my phone and other screens, and transports me to an entirely different world, giving me a break from food-related thoughts and clearing my head.

  Other ideas for you to consider: Listening to a podcast that's nothing to do with food, watching a film (with your phone in the other room), listening to music (again, preferably without your phone), creative writing, playing a board game, crafting, knitting or sewing, practicing a musical instrument, going to a museum or exhibition

- **Home & environment goals:** Your home is an extension of yourself, and the way it looks and feels can make a big difference to your mental wellbeing. Taking care of your home and making your surroundings look nice is therefore an important part of your self-care regime. Small touches that make your home feel more comfortable are a way of looking after yourself and a reminder that you deserve to have nice things in your life. (More on the importance of kindness later.)

  In my case, I love fresh flowers but used to buy them only occasionally. Having gone through the reverse-engineering exercise and identified them as something positive I like having in my life, I now make a point of buying fresh flowers every weekend. I'm not talking huge, expensive bouquets here; just a few seasonal flowers that I place in my living room and my study. (As I am writing this, I am looking at pale yellow carnations on my window sill.) Seeing them simply cheers me up, and I am convinced they help support my general wellbeing.

  Other ideas for you to consider: Tidying up, making your bed in the morning, lighting a scented candle in the evening, cleaning your bathroom and kitchen at regular intervals (such as once a week), changing your sheets, vacuum cleaning, dusting

- **Movement & exercise goals:** Moving your body is an important aspect of your mental and physical wellbeing. You don't need to have a full-blown exercise regime to feel the positive mental health benefits of movement. A regular walk or some stretching would be a perfectly fine starting point. What's key is that you value movement and exercise in their own right, not because you are hoping to lose weight or counter the calories taken in through binging.

I began feeling much better about myself when I started lifting weights, so that is the main focus of my movement goals. I aim to lift weight at least three times a week now. Separately, I sometimes like to set recovery goals around how much stretching and mobility work I do, with the aim of completing at least three fifteen-minute stretching sessions every week.

Other ideas for you to consider: Going for a long walk, getting off one stop early on your commute and walking the rest or parking your car a little farther away, twenty minutes of yoga, doing a group class at the gym, playing with your kids in the park, going for a swim

My Process Goals

I hope the previous section has given you a good starting point for creating your own process goals. Remember, there is a dedicated worksheet to support your goal-setting at the back of the book. For a real-life reference, below are some of the food and non-food actions I came up with early in my recovery, which then formed the basis of my personal process goals. Please take these as inspiration only, and don't be tempted to copy them. It's important you work with goals that are specific to you.

My food-related actions

When I'm in recovery...I eat three meals a day.

When I'm in recovery...I make my coffee at home.

When I'm in recovery...I do my grocery shopping online.

When I'm in recovery...I enjoy a piece of cake on Saturdays.

When I'm in recovery...I bring my lunch to work.

My non-food actions:

When I'm in recovery...I make time to read books.

When I'm in recovery...I lift weights three times a week.

When I'm in recovery...I put my phone away when watching TV.

When I'm in recovery...I wash my hair every day.

When I'm in recovery...I iron my clothes every Sunday.

Finally, once you have defined your own personal process goals, it's a good idea to spend a moment to work out how exactly you are going to keep track of them. In my experience, a simple tracker is the best starting point (though if you love setting up more complicated spreads and trackers in a bullet journal, there's nothing stopping you). If you'd like a template to work from, there's a basic goal tracker form later that you can copy into your recovery journal, or you can download a printable version from www.bingeeatingrecoveryproject.com/worksheets

Recovery Year Dos and Don'ts

With your process goals set, the most important prep for your recovery year is done. However, there are a few more things to consider and put in place before you are ready to kick off the one-year period. The following dos and don'ts will help to clarify what you need to be focused on over the next twelve months, as well as mistakes to avoid.

What To Do

- **Make a formal commitment before you start**, for example by signing a pledge that sets out what you are hoping to learn over the next year. Share it with a friend or family member, if you feel able. (You can find a pledge template you can use at the back of the book and in a printable format at www.bingeeatingrecoveryproject.com/worksheets).

- **Be clear about your priorities.** Your most important goal is not to quit. The biggest risk to your recovery is giving up, so take your time to pick a suitable hero habit and focus your energy on performing it every day. In addition, use process goals to help you develop better food and non-food habits.

- **Plan rewards** for your recovery year. These rewards should recognise and celebrate the fact that you have stuck with the process for a certain amount of time. They should not be tied to how well you think you are doing in your recovery, how much you are binging or what your weight is. Try to have at least one reward planned each month, but feel free to create as many as you like. There's a worksheet later in this book to help you come up with ideas for rewards.

- **Get a single notebook or journal — and stick with it.** If you're anything like me, you'll love the feeling of starting a new journal. All those blank pages always make me feel like a fresh beginning. For your recovery year, however, resist the temptation to start multiple notebooks or journals. Don't rush to buy a new one when you've hit a rocky patch in your recovery and feel like wiping the slate clean. Don't throw a journal away when you've made a mess of your entries or want to try out a new journaling style. Simply turn to a fresh page and continue.

This will teach you how to fight the impulse to cross everything out and start over again. Plus, your journal is an incredibly important record of your recovery that will be full of important insights and lessons by the end of the year. You cannot afford to throw that knowledge away.

- **Capture your thoughts and feelings** at the start of your recovery year. In addition to any tracking or journaling you do as part of your work with self-help books or therapists and coaches, I recommend you write down how you feel as you start your year of recovery, and what your hopes and fears are for the year ahead. You will find it useful to look back at this as your year progresses.

- Once you've started, **keep a continuous record** of what is and isn't working as well as how you are feeling throughout the year. Your recovery year is a fantastic opportunity to learn more about yourself and what kind of self-help advice or therapy you respond well to. Regular journaling is a great way to support that process. It will allow you to gain a deeper understanding of your binge eating patterns and triggers, and provide you with much-needed perspective when you suffer a setback. Remember, journaling doesn't have to be fancy or take up lots of time to be effective.

- **Carefully experiment** with different self-help methods, therapists and coaches. You don't have to do the same thing for the entire year. Feel free to read a range of different books and give therapy or coaching a try. Your recovery doesn't start and end with a particular book or coach; it starts and ends with you. Trying something out and deciding it's not for you is a perfectly legitimate thing to do in your recovery year — provided you are being fair and give each book or coach a decent amount of time before passing judgment.

What Not To Do

- **Don't measure your success by a specific outcome,** such as how much you binge or your weight. Broadly speaking, it's fine for you to monitor how often you binge, but you shouldn't be setting goals based on this.

- **Don't declare your recovery a failure if you experience a setback.** You will suffer setbacks. You will binge again. It's completely normal and doesn't tell you anything about your long-term recovery prospects. Of course, binges are disappointing, but they're not the end of the world. You are still learning the skill of recovery. Don't let a setback freak you out. If you binge, you keep going. If you don't eat as well as you think you should have, you keep going. Focus on your daily process goals and don't quit, no matter what.

- **Don't reward yourself with food** or plan 'cheat meals'. It's completely fine to go for a nice meal during your recovery year or to celebrate a birthday with treats or a bit of overindulgence, but I don't recommend you use food as one of your planned recovery rewards. Instead, challenge yourself to find something non-food related that would bring you joy. For example, I am a bit of a fragrance junkie, so I love using a nice scented candle or a new perfume as one of my rewards. Whatever you do, don't be tempted by the idea of a planned binge or 'cheat meal' to give yourself a break from being 'good'. This is a thoroughly unhealthy way to think about your recovery that will end up harming you physically and mentally.

- **Don't start your recovery year on a Monday** or the first of the month or the start of the new year or some other day that holds particular significance for you. The stars don't need to be aligned in some special way for you to start recovering. All that's needed is your commitment.

- Similarly, **don't try to get a holiday or family occasion out of the way** before you start on your year. Your recovery year is meant to teach you to stay committed no matter what life throws at you, so it's counterproductive to try to tinker with the scheduling to avoid Christmas, Thanksgiving, a big birthday or similar. You'll have to deal with these events sooner or later anyway.

- **Don't jump from one self-help method or coach to the next** without giving them a fair chance. No self-help book or therapist will ever be able to help you if you throw in the towel after a week or skip parts of their programme. You need to give them your full commitment and a decent amount of time before you decide whether they are working for you. If you keep jumping from programme to programme, you will only end up wasting your time. Just as importantly, you should always start by following the advice of your self-help programme or therapist to the letter. You can make adjustments later on, but first give yourself the chance to experience the programme as it's intended. (If necessary, revisit the earlier chapters about how to get the most out of self-help books and therapists.)

- At the same time, **don't be afraid to call time on something that's not working.** Once you have given a programme or therapist a good shot and it's just not working out, it's time to try something new. You are under no obligation to keep going with something that's not helping you. Reflect carefully on why things didn't work out, then draw a line and move on.

OVER TO YOU

The time has come. This is the moment when you choose to commit to spending the next twelve months on your recovery. You are going to give yourself the gift of a full year to get better. A year to improve your understanding of yourself and the factors that drive your binge eating; a year to explore a range of different recovery strategies and tactics to determine what's right for you; a year to lay the foundations for your life after binge eating. Here's your final checklist to make sure you have everything in place:

1) If you haven't done so already, get yourself a notebook or journal that you will use to track your thoughts and progress for the next year. This is your recovery notebook. It doesn't matter what kind of notebook it is. Go with whatever appeals to you, but try to commit to using the same notebook for the entire year. Revisit the section on tracking and journaling for a refresher on some useful techniques.

2) Decide on a hero habit that you can perform every day, no matter what.

3) Use the recovery goals worksheet to define process goals for your recovery year. Try to bear in mind the principles of kaizen and the 1% rule, as described earlier.

4) Plan some rewards for the first three months of your recovery year. Remember these should reward you for sticking with the process and shouldn't be based on whether you've achieved a certain outcome. Use the rewards worksheet for guidance.

5) Complete and sign the recovery pledge and put it somewhere safe. If possible, tell someone you trust about your commit-

ment, but don't worry if you don't feel able to right now. You can progress with your recovery year regardless.

6) Last but not least: Keep reading this book. Indeed, keep reading in general. There is lots more to learn about yourself and how to succeed during your recovery year. Making the initial commitment is just the start.

PILLAR THREE: PRAGMATISM

No amount of self-knowledge is going to help you if you don't know how to apply it. And no amount of time spent on recovery will ever yield results if you can't withstand the realities of everyday life. This is why pragmatism is a crucial recovery skill. **Pragmatism is the lifeblood of recovery.** It's the bridge between knowing what you need to do and actually doing it. It's the glue that holds your recovery together when life throws curveballs at you. And it's the ultimate antidote to all-or-nothing thinking. I truly believe the moment you learn to be pragmatic about your binge eating and your recovery is the moment you start making real progress. So, in this chapter, you will discover:

- The three key **mindset shifts** you need to make to become more pragmatic
- The **hard truths** you need to confront to let go of unrealistic expectations
- How to **overcome food dogma** and embrace pragmatism in your food choices

Three Key Mindset Shifts

Pragmatism, in many ways, is the opposite of perfectionism. Whereas perfectionists tend to obsess about every last detail and won't be satisfied unless everything has gone exactly to plan, pragmatists focus on the **here and now** and take each situation as it comes. Now, I'm not here to tell you how to live your life, and it's certainly not as simple as saying perfectionism is always bad and pragmatism is always good, but when it comes to binge eating pragmatism clearly wins out. That's because binge eating can be a highly capricious problem to deal with, and the recovery journey (as you've learned in previous chapters) is rarely nice and smooth. Under those circumstances, a pragmatic mindset that allows you to adapt to new situations quickly is a real advantage.

Of course, hearing me say this is one thing; actually *believing* that your recovery won't be perfect — and being okay with it — is quite another. I know all too well how easy it is to pay lip service to clichés like 'perfect is the enemy of good' or 'silence your inner critic' without ever seriously challenging your perfectionist tendencies. Luckily, there are simple steps you can take to stop your perfectionism from getting in the way of your recovery. Start by focusing on these three mindset shifts:

- Forget about streaks
- Leave the past in the past
- Stop worrying about forever

No More Streaks

It's very tempting to think in 'streaks' when you start your recovery. *I got three binge-free days in a row!* Indeed, the idea of habit streaks is an important part of several well-known self-improvement programmes. You can get apps to track your streaks. You can even gamify the process and compete against others to see who can maintain the longest habit streak. While this may be helpful in lots of circumstances, I have found it problematic when applied to binge eating. If you are a binge eater, chances are you are already prone to 'all or nothing' thinking and struggle with getting back on track after small setbacks. Pursuing binge-free streaks amplifies those tendencies. Not only have you binged, you've ruined your perfect streak. Somehow that feels much worse.

What's more, thinking in streaks stops you from appreciating whatever you achieved before you broke your streak. If you had a five-day streak of no binges and then you binged on the sixth, you're unlikely to look back at those five days and see them as successes. You'll only see what happened on the sixth day. Of course, that's nonsense. **We don't live our lives in streaks.** Five binge-free days are five binge-free days, regardless of whether they happen to take place in a row. Whatever you achieve today is valid, regardless of what happened yesterday or what might happen tomorrow. If you've managed not to binge today, that's an achievement even if you binge tomorrow.

Don't allow yourself to dismiss what you've achieved because of an arbitrary concept like a streak. Every bit of progress matters. Every binge you avoid is an achievement and teaches you something valuable. It all adds up in the end, streak or no streak.

Leave The Past In The Past

Facing up to the scale of your binge eating problem, and the time and money it's cost you, is an important part of the recovery process. That's why the first few chapters of this book encourage you to ask challenging questions about your binging, and even quantify the damage you've caused yourself. Confronting your binge problem, however, doesn't mean you should spend your days dwelling on past mistakes.

If you find yourself stuck in a loop, constantly reliving every bad food decision you've ever made and wallowing in regret, you'll never get around to actually getting better. Look, **you are where you are.** Your weight is what it is. The food has been eaten. The money has been spent. It's done. Stop beating yourself up over what you could have, should have or might have done differently, and start dealing with the here and now. Of course, intrusive thoughts or regrets about the past won't simply disappear overnight, but you can stop them from dominating your present by:

- Taking a moment whenever you find yourself getting caught up in the past
- Acknowledging your regret over poor choices you made
- But then re-focusing your mind on the present by firmly telling yourself *'This is in the past now; today I am focusing on...'*

This process may not be easy when you first start, but the more you practice interrupting negative thoughts about the past and re-focusing your attention on what you can do today, the easier you'll find it.

But what about *learning* from past mistakes? Doesn't that require a degree of looking back? It's a fair point. To learn lessons and avoid repeating past mistakes you should indeed spend some time analysing what went wrong for you. This, however, needs to happen in a **structured and targeted** manner, with a specific outcome in mind. You'd be looking to answer questions such as, *When do most of your binges occur? What are the circumstances surrounding them? What preventative strategies could you have used during your last binge?*

Critical self-reflection of this kind — including the exercises you were encouraged to pursue in the chapter on self-knowledge — is a far cry from spending hours telling yourself you're a worthless piece of human garbage who's wasted their life and is never going to change. So yes, you should try to learn lessons from the past. But know that you are far more likely to spend *too much* time thinking about the past than too little, and discipline yourself accordingly.

Stop Worrying About Forever

The third important mindset shift you need to make to become more pragmatic is to stop seeing every decision as final and something that commits you for the rest of your life. It probably sounds ridiculous when I put it like this, but it's actually a very common mindset trap for binge eaters to fall into. If you've ever found yourself thinking something like *'I don't want to be the kind of person who has to track their eating forever'*, then you, too, have fallen into this trap.

Because, trust me: **No one is demanding forever.** All the stuff in this and other books, all the stuff you read online, and all the stuff your coach or therapist tells you is there to serve a purpose in your recovery. They are tools for you to use to get better. They do not define who you are for the rest of your life. Don't get me wrong, using recovery tools effectively means you have to commit a decent amount of time to them, but that doesn't mean forever. The most common time frame referenced in this book is thirty days. The longest is a year.

Sure, there may well be some tools that turn into useful long-term habits for you, but many of them aren't designed that way. Many of the tools and techniques you'll encounter during your recovery are specifically designed to be interventions to help you while you're recovering from binge eating. Once you no longer need them, they'll disappear from your life.

So, stop worrying about what using certain recovery tools says about you and your life. Stop worrying about whether your journaling and tracking regime, or your recovery hero habit, or your therapy schedule are things you can keep up forever. You don't have to figure out forever right now. Just take one day at a time.

Hard Truths

I said it in the chapter on time and I'll say it again here: Unrealistic expectations are **poison** for your recovery. They'll make you throw in the towel before you've even started because anything less than perfection will feel like failure.

You've already confronted the biggest unrealistic expectation of them all — that recovery will be quick — but there are a few other hard truths about the recovery process you need to face up to. This won't be much fun, but it's necessary. Positive thinking, motivational pep talks and *'You got this, girl'* inspo all have their place, but they need to be tempered with a dose of reality. Once you understand what the reality of recovery is going to look like — including all the ugly, difficult bits so many chirpy self-help books don't want to tell you about — you can take pragmatic steps to prepare yourself.

You Will Probably Binge Again

Let's get the big one out of the way first: Starting the recovery process most likely won't mean the end of your binges. In all likelihood you are going to binge again. I'm saying *'in all likelihood'* and *'probably'* because there are exceptions to every rule, but it's best to assume you are not going to be the exception. Sorry.

But that's okay. Remember what you learned about kaizen and the 1% rule: You shouldn't try to go from zero to perfect. Most people don't manage to do that. Simply work on getting a little better one step at a time.

The reason I'm so pushy about getting you to confront the fact that binges will still happen is that I didn't understand this for a long time — and it delayed my recovery for years. Sure, I had heard people say recovery doesn't happen overnight and that I might still binge, but I didn't *believe* it. Deep down, I refused to accept this would be true for me. I thought: *'I will be different. I will be the exception to the rule. I will have more discipline and more drive than other people. When I put my mind to it, the binges will stop.'*

Then the inevitable would happen. I would binge. And no matter how much progress I had made until that point, that one binge would **ruin everything**. I was so invested in the idea that recovery equals zero binges that I was incapable of dealing with even the smallest of setbacks. Instead of seeing that binge for what it was — a disappointing but ultimately minor event in the grand scheme of things — I was devastated. I saw it as evidence my entire recovery attempt had been a failure. It clearly hadn't worked, otherwise this binge wouldn't have happened!

Things would spiral out of control from there. Since I had already decided my recovery had failed, there was nothing restraining me from further binges. A single binge would turn into days, weeks and sometimes months of binging. After that, it would take me a long time to even consider another recovery attempt. When I was finally ready to give it another go, I would once again start with that familiar phrase: '*This time it's going to be different.*' And the whole sad cycle would start again.

My point is: The best treatment will fail if you are going to throw it all away the minute you binge. You have to go into this process knowing that binges will still be in your life initially and figure out pragmatic ways to deal with that.

You Probably Won't Lose Weight

At least not while you're in the middle of your recovery from binge eating. I know that's not what you want to hear. I didn't either. I hated the way my body looked after years of binging. Losing weight was the whole purpose of recovery, as far as I was concerned. After all, what was the point of working hard to stop binging if I was still going to end up 'fat' anyway? So, if you're saying weight loss is the one thing that's non-negotiable, the one thing you're not prepared to compromise on, I get it. Seriously.

Unfortunately, the reality is binge eating recovery and weight loss simply aren't goals you can pursue at the same time. They are not complementary. Quite the opposite, in fact. Trying to lose weight will make your binge eating problem worse, not better. The problem is the caloric restriction that's required to achieve weight loss. As you know from the chapter on diets, **restriction is a key factor in binge eating**. If you want to recover from binge eating you can't keep doing the one thing that's driving it. You have to stop dieting and chasing weight loss while you get better.

Is it possible you might lose weight as an unintended side effect during your recovery, simply because you are binging less than before? Sure. For some people this is indeed the case, but for many others stopping the binges doesn't go hand in hand with weight loss. This could be partly because they are keeping their binges in check by eating more during their regular meals or because they already had a tendency to overeat in addition to their binges.

You could be a rare exception to the rule, but there's no way of telling in advance. This is why it makes sense to go into your recovery process assuming you won't be losing any weight. That way, you won't be disappointed.

Now, no one is saying you will never, ever, ever be able to lose weight. All you're being asked to do is to pause your weight loss ambitions while you're recovering. You're already committing to a year of recovery, so **commit to a year of not trying to lose weight**. You need to be pragmatic and deal with your most urgent problem first — your binge eating — before you try to pursue weight-related goals.

I like to think of it this way: Imagine you're an aspiring marathon runner with a broken ankle. Does having a broken ankle mean you'll never run a marathon? Of course not. With the right support and rehab, you can make a full recovery and run that marathon once you're healed up. However, if you jump the gun and try to go for training runs while your ankle isn't fully healed yet, you'll make it worse and set yourself back by months. If you're really unlucky, you may even cause so much damage that you'll never recover fully and your marathon dreams really are over.

You must not chase weight loss goals while your metaphorical ankle is still healing. Give yourself a break from the scales while you're getting better. Deal with your recovery first; think about weight later.

Prepare For Lots Of Trial & Error

During your recovery process, you will come across great books, fantastic self-help programmes and hugely experienced coaches and therapists that will do *nothing* for you. You'll read rave reviews from people who've had life-changing breakthroughs thanks to a certain book or coach — but when you follow the exact same advice, nothing happens. It doesn't mean you've failed; it doesn't mean that book or coach is bad; and it certainly doesn't mean that your binge eating is so terrible that you'll never be cured. It simply means this one thing you tried wasn't right for you. No big deal. There's plenty more for you to try.

Unfortunately, that's not a message you hear very often in self-help or recovery coaching. No one really wants to publish a book or market their coaching services and say: *'I have some interesting thoughts about binge eating that you might find helpful — but you probably want to listen to some other people, too.'* Instead, it's all about *'the definitive take'* or *'the last book you'll ever need to read about binge eating'.*

We've already touched on this in the chapter on self-help, but it bears repeating. Because once you move away from the idea of the one perfect book or the one perfect coach, and you accept you are going to have to look in lots of places to find what's right for you, your attitude towards those books and coaches suddenly becomes much more productive. Instead of asking *'Will this book or coach fix me?'*, your question becomes: *'What can this book or coach teach me that might be useful to me?'*

This is an important mindset shift. Primarily, because **it reduces the pressure**. Right from the start you're saying: *'I know I'm not going to find all the answers here — but I may find something useful that can play a part in my recovery.'* You are telling yourself you're okay with the fact that the book you're reading may not have all the answers. The coach you're seeing doesn't have to be the last coach you'll ever see. This isn't your one and only shot.

What's more, it makes you a more **active participant** in your recovery. By asking *'What can this teach me?'* and picking and choosing what's right for you, you make it your responsibility to find answers instead of sitting back and waiting to be spoon-fed answers someone else has found. Plus, it **stops you from throwing out helpful advice**. If you expect a book or coach to 'fix' you completely — and they don't — you are probably going to dismiss *everything* they have to say. Can't be any good, otherwise you wouldn't still be binging — right?

This is a great way to waste time. You will be missing out on valuable insight if you are not prepared to **judge each piece of advice on its own merit**. The question you should be asking is not *'Has this book or coach cured me?'* but *'What advice do they have to offer that will help me get better long term?'* If the answer is a single paragraph out of a 500-page book — or a single useful exercise out of several coaching sessions — don't dismiss that paragraph or exercise just because the wider package didn't deliver the cure you'd hoped for. Take what's useful to you and look for other answers elsewhere.

You May Not End Up 'Cured'

As I am writing this, I am a couple of years into my recovery from binge eating. I now binge about ten times a year on average. If you've just spat out your coffee and are now furiously googling 'how to get a refund on a book', hear me out.

I realise ten binges a year is probably not what you think success looks like. If I could go back to my old self from, say, five years ago and tell her: *'You'll start this process and it's going to be tough and you'll have to work really hard and at the end you'll still be binging at times,'* she'd have ripped my head off. *'Recovery means no more binges, end of story,'* she'd have told me. *'If you still binge, you've failed.'*

But here's the thing: My old self was an idiot. Back then, I didn't have a clue about what recovery looks like in the real world. I was caught up in wishful thinking and fairy tales about magic cures and overnight recoveries. And, of course, I was a massive fan of 'all or noth-ing' thinking. Needless to say, I also made zero progress. Nada. Zilch. Literally two decades of going around in circles, telling myself I'll never binge again, then binging and starting again from scratch.

Today, on the other hand, I have made lots of progress, even though I've not managed to become binge-free. Let's do a quick calculation. Before my recovery I would spend about four to five months of the year on a super-restrictive diet, and then I'd break down and spend the remaining months pretty much binging full-time. On a conservative es-timate, I'd binge once every three days during those 'bad' months. That equates to sixty to seventy binges a year. (And this was after I'd already left the truly bad days of my teenage years and twenties behind...)

Today I have that figure down to a fraction of that. I have gained be-tween fifty and sixty binge-free days a year. **This is what tangible progress looks like.** I can't stress how much healthier physically and mentally I am as a result of reducing my binges. No, I'm not binge-free, but I would much rather be the current version of myself who's binging ten times a year than the old one who binged seventy times or more.

That's why I believe you stand a much better chance of recovering long term if your initial goal is to make your binge eating *better* rather than becoming completely binge-free. It's too big a jump, in my experi-ence, and you'll become frustrated if you keep failing at it.

That's not to say I don't think you can become binge-free down the line — it's certainly what I'm aiming for. But guess who will be in a bet-ter position to ultimately achieve this? The 'zero tolerance' you who desperately wants to go from full-on binge eater to binge-free in one fell swoop but never actually manages to achieve anything? Or the you that's succeeded in reducing binges and knows how to achieve and sus-tain progress?

Food Pragmatism

So far in this book, I haven't given you any advice on what or how to eat. There are two reasons for this. Firstly, dietary advice for people with disordered eating is a specialist field, and I'm not a specialist. If you think you would benefit from food plans and other nutritional guidance, there are far better people to get that from than me.

Secondly, and more importantly, I don't believe what you eat matters all that much in the grand scheme of things. Nutritional and dietary advice can be helpful in some circumstances, especially if it's been a while since you've had a 'normal' eating routine, but your recovery is going to be far more dependent on **your attitude towards food** than the actual food itself.

We've already touched on the reasons in the sections on food addiction and trigger foods, but it comes down to this: Foods that are triggering or 'problematic' for you are so primarily because you have made a value judgement about them. You've put them on a list of 'forbidden' foods or otherwise designated them as 'bad' and are actively trying to avoid them. In other words, you are restricting — and restriction, of course, is a big factor in binge eating. That is why, in order to develop healthier eating habits, you have to start with tearing up that mental list of 'good' and 'bad' foods. You have to stop being so judgmental about your food choices and develop a more a pragmatic attitude to food.

How do you do that? It starts with being able to resist food dogma.

Resisting Food Dogma

By food dogma I mean statements about food, diet and eating that are presented as **absolute truths**, regardless of circumstance. That probably sounds extreme, though the ideology and belief systems behind food dogma often aren't extreme at all. They can be pretty reasonable, in fact. There may even be good scientific or other evidence to support them. This is an important point because people hear 'food dogma' and they think 'crazy'. They think extreme diets and wildly unscientific claims. And they also think: *'This is pretty obvious stuff and I'm not going to be taken in.'*

But food dogma doesn't have to be extreme to be damaging. Perfectly sensible statements like *'We should all be trying to eat more home-cooked meals and less processed food'* or *'When buying meat, choosing grass-fed or free-range is the most ethical choice'* can turn just as toxic as more outlandish claims. What makes dogmatic thinking problematic isn't the substance behind the thought, but how rigidly you apply it.

Recovery from binge eating is complex, difficult and often messy. To make it through the process successfully, flexibility is going to be your number one ally. You will need to be nimble and able to respond quickly to changing circumstances. If you are wedded to certain dogmatic thoughts about how you should be eating — no matter how well-intentioned or sensible in theory — you are going to struggle to make the right, pragmatic decisions for your recovery when needed.

Easing Up On Nutrition Ambition

One particularly common way dogmatic views can interfere with recovery is the idea of 'healthy eating'. Many of us think binge eating recovery and healthy eating are inextricably linked. However, **recovery from binge eating doesn't require textbook nutrition.** It is entirely possible for you to recover successfully while eating in a way that would not be considered 'healthy' in the traditional sense. You can be low on your fruit and veg intake, not get enough protein, skimp on your whole grains or eat sugar and processed convenience foods, and still get a grip on your binging.

Don't get me wrong: It's perfectly sensible for you to want to eat healthily and nourish yourself with nutritious foods, but that's a separate goal from not binging. The two are not the same, nor does one require the other. In fact, being too preoccupied with healthy eating and nutrition can actively hinder your recovery. Even concepts like mindful or intuitive eating can be problematic because they can encourage you to over-think your food choices and fall into the diet-masquerading-as-healthy-lifestyle trap that leads to restriction and, in the end, more binging. As a binge eater in recovery, you don't want to be in a position where you can fall off any kind of food wagon, even if it's a very benign-sounding mindful eating wagon.

What's more, a preoccupation with healthy eating principles or a certain style of eating can stop you from doing what's right for you while you're going through recovery. Let me give you an example.

The Art Of Compromise

The place where I work has a cafeteria I never used to go to because I thought it sold cheap, stodgy, low-nutrition food. Instead, I would bring a meal-prepped, home-cooked lunch to work every day. Now, there is no doubt in my mind that the lunches I made myself were vastly superior to the cafeteria stuff. In fact, I am willing to bet they were better on pretty much every nutrition metric, from salt, sugar and fat content to protein vs carb ratios as well as overall food production standards, provenance, welfare and other quality indicators.

However, they also took up an enormous amount of my time. I used to spend the best part of my weekend prepping my lunches for the week. I spent even more time researching recipes and scrolling through meal prep #inspo. I knew this level of obsession was bad for me, but I was also stuck on the idea that meal prepping was a good habit; something I *should* be doing, and something that would help me be healthy, while buying cafeteria sandwiches would make me unhealthy. All the while, of course, I kept on binging anyway and made virtually no progress with my recovery.

It took me a long time to realise that although I agreed with the principles of meal prepping, it was not a helpful habit during that stage of my recovery. Once I stopped meal-prepping and bought lunch from the cafeteria instead, the difference was remarkable. Instead of agonising for hours over what to meal-prep for the week, I would take a look at what was on the menu that day, make a snap decision, buy my lunch — and done. Sure, I would end up eating sandwiches made with industrial white bread and heavily processed ham on some days. Or soups that probably came out of giant vats and were crazily high in salt. But the amount of mental space and freedom I gained as a result of this simple, pragmatic intervention was a price worth paying — for that moment at least.

Because I didn't end up buying cafeteria lunches forever. After a few weeks, I had enough and craved going back to my meal prepping routine. So that's what I did. And when that got too much again, I went back to buying cafeteria lunches once more.

A Break From The Big Questions

This is what food pragmatism is all about. You focus on what's right for you **at that particular stage of your recovery**, not some abstract principles about how you think you should be eating in an ideal world. Instead of asking big, abstract questions like *'Is meal prepping good?'*, you ask *'Is meal prepping a good habit for me right now?'* Instead of worrying about whether you are eating too much sugar or not enough fruit and vegetables, you consider whether focusing on reducing sugar or eating more fruit and veggies is helpful to you *right now*.

If the answer is no then don't do it, no matter how much you agree with the underlying idea. Food principles and habits like meal prepping shouldn't define who you are as a person; they are tools in a toolbox for you to pick up and use when they suit your needs — and to put away when they don't.

Similarly, if an 'unhealthy' habit, such as buying cafeteria sandwiches, convenience meals, sugary snacks or processed foods, makes it easier for you to manage your binge eating right now, then don't feel guilty about it. **Give yourself permission to compromise on your food principles** and healthy eating ambitions for the sake of your recovery.

As we already discussed, no one is saying you'll have to do this forever. We're not talking about the rest of your life here. You'll have plenty of time to stick to your principles and food ethics later. But you need to get a handle on your binge eating first. Right now, **the biggest risk to your health is your binge eating.** Forget about cutting out processed foods or not eating as much sugar. Forget about going gluten-free, dairy-free, low-carb or high-fat. All that stuff is window dressing if you are still binging. The single biggest improvement you can make to your long-term health is reducing your binges. That's why the focus of your recovery needs to be on whatever it takes to achieve that. If it means putting on hold your healthy eating ambitions for a little while, so be it.

What About Food Ethics?

We've largely talked about healthy eating principles in this chapter, but I understand that certain ethical concerns, such as the use of animal products, welfare systems or environmental footprints, can make it difficult for some people to 'ease up' on their food choices. Having said that, I believe it's important to point out that food ethics which massively restrict what you can and can't eat are potentially problematic for binge eaters — even if there is no caloric restriction or weight loss goal involved.

Just think about the level of planning that's required to stick to, say, a vegan diet, compared with a standard diet. How frequently you have to check food labels to make sure you don't eat a forbidden ingredient. How much research you have to do to find appropriate recipes. How you have to check restaurant menus in advance to make sure you can order something that's compliant. Never mind the potential health benefits, ethical advantages or sustainability credentials; as a binge eater, the level of thinking, planning and checking involved in a diet like that should make you think twice.

I believe you need to be particularly careful if you are considering switching to an ethically driven eating style (such as veganism) *during* your recovery. Make sure you are clear and honest with yourself about your motives, and that you are not dressing up urges to restrict as ethical choices. Part of your disorder is a tendency to obsess about food. Before you adopt a new style of eating, you should therefore ask yourself: '*Will this support my recovery goals and make me more pragmatic in my food choices — or will I end up spending more time thinking and worrying about food?*'

OVER TO YOU

1) Write down three examples of food dogma that you've encountered in your life, and that you are committing to challenging during your recovery year. There's a worksheet later to guide you through the process.

2) Think back to the three mindset shifts we discussed at the start of the chapter. How might these help you challenge the food dogma you've just identified?

3) Revisit the section on hard truths about binge eating recovery. Which of those truths scare you the most? Why? Write down your feelings in as much detail as possible, then come up with at least three actions you are going to take to challenge your fears.

4) Think of a recent binge you had. How might pragmatism and the principles you learned about in this chapter have helped you in that situation?

PILLAR FOUR: KINDNESS

Binge eating is an exhausting problem to have, and the recovery process can be equally exhausting. There are self-help books to read, therapists and coaches to see, exercises to do, journals to write in and checklists to tick off. So much of what you do and think about ends up revolving around your binge eating problem and whether you're doing well in your recovery. Sometimes this can feel like you're stuck in a permanent performance appraisal, and the only thing that matters in your life is whether you've managed not to binge.

Of course, that's not true. Your value as a human being doesn't come down to what happens with your binging. Binge eating isn't a moral failing you have to atone for, though it can often feel that way. This is why it's **important to make time to be kind to yourself**, both emotionally and physically. You need to remind yourself that you deserve to be loved and respected as you are. You don't need to prove yourself worthy by not binging. So, in this chapter, we'll cover:

- How to approach **kindness and self-care** during your recovery
- How **small acts** such as changing the clothes you wear can make a big difference to how you feel about yourself
- And how to be kind to yourself — and move on — when you experience **setbacks**

The Importance Of Self-Care

Let's start by exploring what being kind to yourself might look like in practice. Self-care has become a bit of a buzzword topic recently and can mean anything from daily meditation to taking a break from social media or running a bath. These are all perfectly valid options, by the way, but the exact specifics aren't my focus here. I want to share with you some broader, more general thoughts on how to approach self-care, which will work with whatever you end up putting into your personal self-care routine.

The first important point is that, whatever you do as part of your self-care routine, you're setting aside a specific block of time that's purely for you. **Self-care isn't something you should try to multi-task.** Personally, I also believe true self-care should not involve anything that pushes you outside of your comfort zone. I know some people say things like *'Eating healthily and exercising is the kindest thing you can do for yourself'*, but I think they are missing the point. If something doesn't come easily to you, whether it's eating healthily or going to the gym, I don't think you should try to convince yourself it's part of your self-care. Leave the challenging self-improvement stuff for some other time. Your self-care time should be when you indulge yourself *as you are*. Stay within your comfort zone and make it extra comfy.

Avoiding Negative Self-Talk

Importantly, being kind to yourself is so much more than a specific self-care routine. It starts with listening carefully to the voice in your own head. Are you regularly telling yourself things like:

- *I'm fat.*
- *Everything I wear looks awful on me.*
- *I'm weak, greedy and disgusting.*
- *Why can't I be like a normal person?*

If any of these sound remotely familiar, your self-care and kindness routine needs to start with sorting out that voice in your head, before you worry about any of the more stereotypical 'self-care' stuff. Your own voice is the one you hear the most, and what you tell yourself has real impact on your mental health — and your chances of recovery. You need to make sure you have something kind and supportive to say. Try not to berate yourself for what you perceive to be your shortcomings, or constantly pass judgment on your choices, food-related or otherwise.

Of course, negative thoughts aren't something you can just switch off, but you can help keep them in check by being very **deliberate about noticing** them. If you catch yourself engaging in negative self-talk, take a moment, really notice what you're doing and then try to direct your mind towards something more positive.

Negative self-talk is especially common — and damaging — when it relates to your body, so be particularly vigilant on that front. For example, if you find yourself constantly checking your appearance, it might be helpful to **cover up the mirrors in your house** for a while. I've done this at various points in my recovery and it helped me realise just how often I look at my body, without even noticing.

Another self-care tactic I've found useful is making a point of buying nice things for myself. I'm not saying consumerism is the answer to low self-worth or binge eating, but I believe it's important you are willing to indulge yourself a little. This is especially true because, as binge eaters, we are often desperate to lose weight, so there can be a tendency to want to delay spending money on ourselves. Instead, we hold out until we've transformed into a new and improved (and, of course, much smaller) version of ourselves. It's important to challenge this. **You deserve to have nice things in your life right now.** You don't need to wait. You only have this one life and you never know what's around the corner. Don't deprive yourself of joy and pleasure.

Let's Talk About Clothes

One especially egregious form of denying yourself pleasure is wearing clothes that don't fit. It's such an unbelievably pointless exercise that I'm still amazed at how many years — decades! — I spent doing it. Forcing your body into clothes that are too small literally achieves nothing except for making you miserable. You look bad, you feel horrible and you're not impressing anyone (news flash: no one cares about the tag inside your clothes).

So why do we do it? A mixture of denial, wishful thinking and a whopping dose of self-loathing, in my experience. We don't want to 'waste' money on bigger clothes because we're going to lose all that weight anyway. We think buying bigger clothes means we're 'giving up', but keeping the old ones will motivate us. We feel there's no point buying anything new because whatever we wear looks crap on us anyway.

This kind of thinking is hugely unhelpful. You deserve to be comfortable and wear clothes that fit your body *as it is today.* Don't deny yourself this basic human comfort.

There's another, important reason why you should stop wearing clothes that are too small for you. I believe you need to consider the possibility that the act of constantly wearing ill-fitting clothes can be **triggering in its own right**. It's not good for your mental wellbeing to squeeze yourself into clothes that constrict you and leave you barely able to breathe. That's not motivating. It's cruel and humiliating, and it may actively harm your chances of recovery.

Buying new clothes doesn't have to involve spending a fortune either. You don't need an extravagant new wardrobe, if that's not something you can afford or want to commit to. Buy a few basics to begin with.

Creating A Recovery Capsule

I have found the concept of **a capsule wardrobe** a helpful tool in this regard. A capsule wardrobe is, essentially, a curated collection of clothes. The idea is that, instead of having a wardrobe full of random stuff that you never wear, you limit the number of items and make sure everything in your wardrobe is something that you like and — importantly — fits you. Some people create capsule wardrobes for different seasons or occasions, such as a spring capsule or 'going out' capsule. If you search for 'capsule wardrobe' on Google or YouTube, you'll find lots of examples.

What I did is create a recovery capsule. I went out and bought a small number of items **in my actual size**, so I could be comfortable at work and at home. I bought shirts and blouses that didn't stretch dangerously across my boobs and were constantly gaping open, and trousers that didn't feel like they might rip at any point. I bought comfortable loungewear and gym clothes that weren't see-through because the Lycra was stretched so tight. Most importantly, I bought some underwear that didn't feel like a tourniquet and left me with red welts all over my body. (If you only buy one thing, I recommend you make it underwear. It makes a big difference.)

I didn't spend a huge amount of money on my recovery capsule, because you don't need a capsule full of pricey investment pieces. You simply need some stuff that fits you right now. What I learned during this process was this: Calling this collection of clothes my recovery capsule wardrobe made it much easier for me to admit I needed new (and bigger) clothes. Suddenly it no longer felt like I was replacing my wardrobe *forever*. I was simply creating a capsule for a particular period in my life, which I would be at liberty to retire once I no longer needed it.

This is so important. Buying bigger sizes today doesn't say anything at all about what might happen with your weight in the future. All it says is that you care enough about yourself, your body and your mental health *as they are today* to not punish yourself with bad, restrictive clothes.

Body Positivity

While we're on the subject of clothes and body size, let's spend a brief moment discussing body positivity and body acceptance. In essence, body-positive thinking encourages people to accept and embrace the body they have instead of trying to change it. This can mean embracing a larger body than society deems acceptable, but it can also apply to different abilities, the aging process or skin conditions like acne. The emphasis is on promoting overall health and wellbeing instead of a specific aesthetic outcome. Movements like fat acceptance and health at every size (HAES) are often allied to body positivity.

The body-positive movement has had a huge impact in recent years on how we think and talk about body weight and size. As far as binge eating is concerned, it has played a significant role in calling out diet culture and the way it pushes people towards restrictive eating patterns which, in turn, contribute towards binge eating. It has also encouraged the emergence of a new wave of body-positive eating disorder therapists and anti-diet dietitians, who are approaching binge eating treatment in ways that can be quite different (and refreshing) from traditional therapy and recovery programmes.

If you have been heavily fixated on trying to lose weight and feel nervous about the idea of not pursuing weight loss during your recovery period, then finding a body-positive therapist or educating yourself on body positivity and its core concepts could be helpful.

At the same time, **it's also perfectly alright if the body-positive movement doesn't resonate with you.** Not everything is for everyone. The same rules apply to body-positive thinking as to anything else: Evaluate it critically, test it out, see what works for you, and don't feel obliged to keep going if it's not right for you.

In my own case, I see body positivity as a hugely positive influence overall, and I have learned a lot about the role of diet culture in perpetuating binge eating problems. It's one of the reasons I recommend you put your own weight loss on ice for a minimum of a year. I believe body-positive advocates are absolutely right when they warn against weight loss goals fuelling the diet-binge cycle. Yet I also still want to change my body. Not right now and perhaps not for a while — I've learned my lesson and understand binge eating recovery and weight loss can't happen at the same time. However, I won't lie to you and tell you I am totally happy with how I look. That's simply not the reality of the situation for me. Instead, my own body acceptance is very pragmatic. I accept I can't focus on losing weight while I remain vulnerable to binging, and I have learned not to be distraught because of it — but that doesn't mean I have to like it.

Feeling this way doesn't make me a failure or a sad victim of diet culture who needs to wake up and accept herself for who she is. It simply makes me a person with different views and different needs in some areas. The same applies to you. **You are not beholden to any one ideology or school of thought.** You are not required to become a body-positivity convert in order to recover from binge eating. Your choice isn't 'six-week bikini body' fads on the one hand and total body love on the other.

You are allowed to have shades of grey in how you feel about yourself. You are allowed to be conflicted. You are even allowed to want to lose weight. It's not a crime. (Though, as we've discussed at length, it's important you don't act on those wishes while you're still mid-recovery.) There's nothing kind about telling yourself that anything other than unconditional body love is a failure. If that's not where you are right now, give yourself a break. You're under enough pressure already.

Forgiving Yourself After A Setback

One final, important aspect of being kind to yourself is learning how to forgive yourself after a setback. This is one of the most valuable recovery skills you can have. The reality is, setbacks are a normal part of recovering. They happen to all of us, and they will happen to you. However, they don't need to derail your recovery if you know how to deal with them.

As I explained earlier, the process starts with accepting that you will most likely binge again, even if your recovery is going brilliantly. No progress will be possible until you're clear on that. Of course, accepting the reality of setbacks doesn't mean you won't be disappointed when they happen. At times a setback will feel truly devastating, especially if you had been doing well in the run up to it.

When this happens, it's useful to **have a plan for how to get back on track**. Before we dive into some ideas for you to try, let me stress an important point. Having a post-binge strategy doesn't mean you're tempting fate or creating a self-fulfilling prophecy, and it doesn't mean you're planning to binge either. It simply means you're being rational. You're being a grown-up about recovery because you know it's not the setback itself that dooms a recovery attempt; it's how you react to it.

Five Ways to Minimise The Impact Of A Binge

- **Write a letter to your future self.** In the heat of the moment, when you've just been hit by an unexpected binge, it can be hard to remain calm and have a sense of perspective. This is where a letter to yourself, written in advance, can help. It should be a kind, compassionate letter, containing all the things you need to hear when you're at your lowest. Don't be harsh or tell yourself off. This isn't the time for tough love. Instead, remind yourself of how far you've come and why this recovery is important to you. Encourage yourself to draw a line and get back on track. You might also want to include a quote or picture that is meaningful to you or inspires you. Put your letter in a safe space and read it after you had a binge or some other type of setback. You will be surprised by how much it helps.

- **Create a back-on-track ritual.** A ritual can help you draw a line under your binge and signal that you're ready to move on. It doesn't have to be anything fancy. It can be something as simple as taking a shower, putting on a comfortable piece of clothing or lighting a scented candle. Whatever you choose, make sure it's something you can do *no matter what*. Special props or ingredients that you may not always have to hand can quickly turn into an excuse for not moving on. I also strongly recommend you focus your ritual on something other than food. Having special post-binge foods — especially anything that is supposedly cleansing or detoxing — can be dangerous. My own back-on-track ritual has varied over the years, but it usually starts with taking a big rubbish bag, collecting all the food detritus and empty packaging, and throwing them out into the trash. If at all possible, I then have a shower and wash my hair. Scent is very important to me and can really change my mood, so I also like to apply some treatment fragrance or aromatherapy oil to my wrists and temples as part of my ritual.

- **Don't punish yourself.** The single most effective strategy for minimising the impact of a binge is making sure a single binge doesn't turn into lots of binges. This means you have to avoid restricting food at all cost. Restriction, as we discussed earlier, is what fuels binges, so if you attempt to starve yourself or reduce your normal food intake to compensate for a binge, you are setting yourself up for more binges. It's also a heartbreakingly brutal way to treat yourself. Your body is in enough distress already; don't make it worse by depriving it of food. Drink plenty of fluids (if you've binged on processed foods high in sugar and salt, you'll feel very dehydrated) and then eat your next meal just as you normally would. Don't skip anything. Don't fast. Don't 'detox'. None of these will undo a binge. What is done is done. The best thing you can do is be kind to yourself and move on. Similarly, don't make yourself go to the gym or try to burn off your binge calories through physical activity. Exercise should be something you do to take care of yourself, not a punishment you inflict.

- **Talk to someone.** The immediate period after a binge can be a very lonely time. You feel disgusted, ashamed and full of regret. Reaching out and speaking to someone is probably the last thing you'll want to do, but it's also one of the most helpful things. Talking to another person takes the binge out of your head and makes it real. It happened — but now you're moving on. Ideally, decide in advance who you are likely to talk to in the event of a binge and discuss with them how they can help you. You might want to share some of what you have written in your letter to yourself to help guide them, or you can simply ask them to listen or sit with you so you're not alone.

- **Reflect and learn.** A binge is an important opportunity for you to learn about yourself. As soon as you feel able to, sit down with your recovery journal and look back at what happened. How were you feeling that day? What were your stress levels like? Where were you in your cycle? What were you doing immediately before the binge started? Was there an event that you think triggered you? And, importantly, what do you think you will do differently next time? There's a worksheet at the back of the book, to support you in your reflection, which is also available as a free printable download at www.bingeeatingrecoveryproject.com/worksheets. The important point is that you challenge yourself to be analytical about your binging, even if you're thinking *'What's the point? This is just what I do.'* Sometimes patterns only become apparent when you take the time to look for them.

One More Big Mindset Shift

I want to leave you with a final thought that has helped me be kinder to myself during my recovery. Instead of thinking of binges as mistakes you are personally responsible for, try to think of them more as bouts of illness. Something like catching a cold, for example. Colds are annoying, for sure. They make you feel run-down and cranky, and sometimes they can ruin your plans.

But you don't blame yourself when you catch a cold. You don't berate your body for not having been strong enough to withstand the cold virus. You don't force yourself to stand in the pouring rain to teach your stupid, lazy, cold-loving body a lesson. Instead, you look after yourself. You know instinctively that this is a delicate time for your body, and you do your best to give it a helping hand. You treat yourself to chicken soup and steaming cups of tea, and then you tuck yourself in warm and get plenty of rest.

Imagine what your experience of binging would be like if you were as kind to yourself — and to your body — after a binge as you are when you have a cold. Imagine if you saw your binges not as personal failures but cries for help from a body that's run down and in need of some TLC. Imagine if your first instinct after a binge were not punishment, but kindness. I am willing to bet the setbacks wouldn't feel nearly as bad as they do now — and you would emerge from your 'cold' well-rested, stronger and more resilient than before.

OVER TO YOU

1) Brainstorm three ideas for how you might start building a self-care routine for yourself. They don't need to be fully formed at this stage — even committing to reading more about self-care or getting ideas from articles or books counts. Just make sure you capture at least three actionable ideas in your journal.

2) Think of the three worst things you've said or thought about yourself. Imagine you're a lawyer or public defender, and it's your job to defend yourself against these charges. What would you say in your defence? How would you prove the things you've said about yourself to be wrong?

3) Write a letter of forgiveness and encouragement to yourself. It doesn't have to be long. Be generous, understanding and kind about your setbacks and failings, and unwavering in your encouragement and support.

4) Revisit the section on dealing with setbacks and minimising the impact of a binge and create the back-on-track ritual described there.

5) Buy one item of clothing that fits you at the size you are today — even if it's just some new underwear. (Shoes and accessories don't count.)

PILLAR FIVE: MENTAL SPACE

Recovery involves lots of reflection. Whether you are working with a therapist or using self-help, recovery programmes are full of prompts and cues encouraging you to think critically about your binge eating problem, investigate its roots and causes, analyse its patterns, reflect on progress, and so on and so forth. At various points in your recovery process, you may be required to keep a food diary, track and log habits, conduct regular review sessions or try journaling.

This is important work that will help you better understand your binge eating — and therefore make you better equipped to tackle it. However, thinking about your binges shouldn't turn into a full-time job. This is especially true as binge eaters already have a tendency to obsess about food. It's part and parcel of our condition. If you find yourself tracking and analysing your eating patterns and food habits all day long, it's time to take a step back and think about creating some mental space away from food. In this chapter you are going to discover a number of strategies to help you achieve this. In particular, you will learn:

- Why it's important to **schedule dedicated blocks of time** to think about your recovery, and what to do during those blocks
- How to **reset your social media** to help support your recovery
- How to **rediscover interests** and hobbies away from food

- How a **recovery reading list** can give you new ideas while minimising the time you spend thinking about food and binging

Scheduling Food Thinking Time

A good way to start creating more mental space is by becoming more deliberate about when you think about food and for how long. By setting aside a dedicated block of time for food thoughts, you will avoid getting too caught up dwelling on your binges and eating habits. Whether it's daily, weekly or monthly, schedule a set amount of time to think about your binge eating. This is when all your binge reflections, food analysis, reviews and journaling, as required by your therapist or self-help programme, should take place.

When deciding how long these blocks should be, err on the side of short. As a starting point, think ten to twenty minutes for daily sessions; thirty to sixty minutes for weekly; and no more than two hours for a monthly session. Remember, the overarching goal here is to free up mental space and **spend less time thinking about food and eating**. If you find yourself straying outside your allocated block, stop and remind yourself there's a specific time in your schedule for that. You may also want to experiment with creating a ritual around those time blocks (even something as simple as making a cup of tea) to solidify the idea of dedicated food thinking time in your mind. Here are two more important principles:

- **Have a clear agenda for each block of thinking time.** The time you spend thinking about your binge eating and food habits should be constructive — that is, it should serve a purpose. There is little to be gained from aimlessly dwelling on your binging. If anything, it will make you feel worse. Instead, approach each block of time with an agenda. This could be a specific task you need to complete (such as a food journal entry or review session) or a question you want to answer (such as

'What time of day do most of my binges take place?'). Write down your agenda for each thinking block in advance and commit to staying focused on it throughout. Once you have completed your task or answered your question, bring the thinking time to a close and move on with your day.

- **Gradually space out thinking blocks.** At different points in your recovery, you may require daily, weekly or monthly blocks of thinking time. Some recovery programmes, for example, like you to keep a daily food log at the beginning of the process, to help you better understand your eating and binging patterns. Go along with whatever your self-help programme or therapist recommends, but over time you may find it helpful to reduce the frequency of your thinking blocks. In many cases this will happen naturally. Once you have a good handle on your eating and binging patterns, for instance, you may find you naturally progress to weekly as opposed to daily thinking blocks. The key point to remember is that just because you started with daily, weekly or monthly thinking blocks doesn't mean you're required to stick with them forever. It's normal for your thinking time needs to change as you progress through different stages of your recovery. Keep doing what you're doing as long as it works for you, then reassess.

Resetting Your Social Media

How much of the social media you consume every day is in some way related to food, weight or body image? How many healthy recipe ideas do you see? How many inspirational quotes about body positivity? How many fitness journeys? How many 'before' and 'after' pictures? How much food porn? How many critiques of diet culture?

If you're anything like I used to be, you're probably drowning in this stuff without even realising. It was only when I made a point of auditing my social media that I saw that nearly all of it was in some way related to food. No books, no music, no art, no culture, no travel. The things I thought I was interested in were barely represented. Instead, it seemed like food and other people's bodies were the only things I cared about. If this sounds familiar, it's time to take action. The average person spends 135 minutes a day on social media, so if your social feeds are filled with food and body content you are spending a big chunk of your day looking at food and bodies. You are quite literally curating a version of reality in which food and bodies are the only things everyone thinks and talks about.

Of course, that's not the case. People have all sorts of other interests. Some don't spend any time at all thinking about food and bodies. (*Just imagine!*) This is the version of the world you need to be spending more time in. Enter the **social media reset**. In the extreme version, I would tell you to go through the accounts, boards and hashtags you follow, and unfollow or mute anything and anyone to do with food and body image. But I understand that can be quite a jump — at least initially. So, ease your way in. Carefully review who you follow and see if you can identify where most of the food and body-related content comes from. Then **commit to muting those accounts for thirty days**. Once those thirty days are up, review and decide whether you missed those accounts. If you did, and you feel they are not compromising your ability to recover, then feel free to follow or unmute them again.

As you do this, it's important you bear in mind that some accounts might be entertaining, yet still harmful to your recovery. Even content that is positive and supportive about binge eating or body image can fill up your mental space with constant ideas about food, weight and body image, when obsessive thoughts about food, weight and body image are precisely what you're trying to fight.

Remember, you are so much more interesting than this binge eating problem you have. You are so much more than your body. There are so many more interesting things you could be spending your time thinking about other than food. Find those and fill your social feeds up with them instead.

Cultivating Non-Food Interests

Like many mental health conditions, binge eating can make you lose touch with who you really are. It overshadows your true self. This is why digging out the real person underneath the binges and the obsessive food thoughts is such an important part of recovery. Rediscovering old interests and developing new ones will help you see **there is life beyond binge eating**. It will also help to distract you from unhelpful thoughts about food and body weight.

Start by setting some time aside, take your journal and ask yourself the following questions:

- What was your biggest passion when you were a child?
- Are there any past hobbies you might want to rekindle?
- What have you always wanted to try?
- What's a skill you've always wanted to learn?
- What skills or interests do you admire in others?
- What was the last book you read and what did you like about it? Is there something in there that you might want to cultivate into a wider interest?
- What about the last film or TV show you saw?

Don't fret if you don't immediately come up with answers. Give yourself some time to reflect and write down ideas as and when they come to you. Don't worry at this stage if they are realistic or if you have the time or money to do them. Allow your imagination to run free. By the same token, your ideas don't have to be anything big. You don't need to find lots of new, expensive hobbies. Cultivating non-food interests can be about identifying small things that are meaningful to you and hold your interest, whether it's listening to music, reading a novel, trying out a new class at the gym, visiting a museum or watching a show on Netflix. Go with whatever appeals to you.

Once you have collected a few ideas, review them and **pick the easiest option on your list**. Commit to spending a small amount of time on this activity every week for the next month. For example, you might decide to spend half an hour once a week reading a novel. It really doesn't have to be any more complicated or dramatic than that.

After the first month, expand the time you spend on your new activity or add more activities, if you feel comfortable. There is no right or wrong here, provided what you do takes your head to a different place and gives you a break from constantly thinking about food.

Creating A Recovery Reading List

One final, important way in which you can reclaim some mental space is to change your reading habits. This strategy works regardless of whether you are much of a reader at the moment or not. The idea is quite straightforward: You put together a special recovery reading list that **deliberately exposes you to new ideas** and helps to distract you from obsessive thoughts about food, and then you commit to spending a certain amount of time each week reading. It doesn't have to be a huge amount of begin with. Even half an hour will make a difference.

As the brilliant Matt Haig writes in Notes On A Nervous Planet: *'Reading isn't important because it helps to get you a job. It's important because it gives you room to exist beyond the reality you're given.'*

Your recovery reading could come from books as well as articles, though I would encourage you towards books if at all possible. They tend to be more immersive and therefore more effective at taking you away from thoughts about food and eating. Plus, they give you a break from the hectic, short-attention-span kind of reading that tends to happen when we read articles online. It doesn't matter if you read your books in paperback or on a digital device like a Kindle.

As for what kinds of books should be on your recovery reading list, there's only one rule: They should have **nothing whatsoever to do with binge eating** or food in general. I am, of course, not suggesting you shouldn't read books about binge eating. I am simply suggesting you also need to do other kinds of reading — and the special time you are setting aside here should be reserved only for that.

If you are looking for some guidance on what to choose, I have a few recommendations you might find helpful. First, I recommend you put **both fiction and non-fiction** books on your list. I really believe in the power of fiction to take you out of your head for a while. If you are not a frequent fiction reader at the moment, you might find reading novels hard-going at first, but it's a habit worth persisting with. I always find I am calmer and less impulsive when I maintain a regular fiction reading habit. When choosing fiction books, go with whatever appeals to you and don't be afraid to experiment. If you've never been much of a crime fiction, romance or fantasy reader, you may be surprised by how much you enjoy them. And if something doesn't turn out to be right for you, don't be afraid to put the book down and move on to something else. There are thousands more books for you to discover and enjoy.

On the non-fiction side, I recommend a slightly more deliberate approach. If a subject matter is greatly appealing to you (and provided it meets the important rule on not being binge eating or food-related), then there's nothing stopping you from adding it to your reading list, of course. In addition to that, however, I suggest you also seek out non-fiction and self-help books that explore **specific skills** that could be useful to you in your recovery.

Many of the problems we encounter as binge eaters are, in fact, problems other people encounter too; they just don't happen to manifest those problems through binge eating. We all have our own struggles and want to figure out how to lead better, happier, more fulfilled lives. By reading books that seek to answer some of those questions — but in a way that's not focused on food — you can gain new perspectives on your own challenges, without having to spend yet more time reading self-help about binge eating. Here are five of my favourite books that have done this for me:

- **Notes On A Nervous Planet** by Matt Haig is inspired by Haig's experience with depression and anxiety, which he has turned into a brilliant 'how to' guide on keeping your sanity in the 21st century. Written in a very accessible and easy to read style, it's full of thought-provoking prompts and ideas that will make you look at the small things in life in a new light. Aside from the quote about the importance of reading I mentioned previously, I also really like this one: *'Remember no one really cares what you look like. They care what they look like. You are the only person in the world to have worried about your face.'*

- **Grit** by Angela Duckworth is a fascinating exploration of perseverance that asks: *What makes some people so good at pursuing their goals with complete focus, while others flit aimlessly from one thing to the next?* The difference has nothing to do with talent but is down to a skill all of us can learn, argues psychologist Duckworth. The powerful skill of grit. As she says in one of my favourite quotes from the book: *'Enthusiasm is common. Endurance is rare.'*

- **Essential Zen Habits** by Leo Babauta is the book version of key insights from Babauta's hugely popular Zen Habits blog, which explores what it takes to lead a happy life — and what kinds of habits and everyday practices will help you get there. Containing practical advice on how to create new habits and make them stick, as well as thoughts on mindfulness and breaking behavioural patterns that are hurting you, I have found this a really refreshing (and quick to read) take on habit building. Babauta's earlier book on minimalism — called The Power Of Less — is also worth a look.

- **Wait But Why, Year One** by Tim Urban is another book that started out as a blog. In fact, it's basically an e-book version of Urban's brilliant Wait But Why blog. And I cannot stress how brilliant it is — WBW is probably my favourite blog of all time. It explores a huge range of subjects, from procrastination to how to stop caring about what other people think, in a truly unique and entertaining style (featuring some brilliant illustrations). Before buying the book, I'd recommend reading a couple of posts on Urban's blog first to make sure it's a style you enjoy, preferably starting with his two-parter on Why You Procrastinate.

- **Get Your Sh*t Together** by Sarah Knight is one of several no-nonsense books written by Knight about how to take charge of your life and stop worrying about what other people might think of you. Her style isn't for everyone (as the title suggests, there's plenty of swearing), but I have found her books to be full of good advice and an effective jolt to the system when you need to break out of a rut. Some of my favourite quotes of hers include: *'Proven fact: You can never finish something you didn't start'* and *'Big life changes are made in small, manageable chunks.'*

OVER TO YOU

1) Identify one fiction and one non-fiction book that you are going to read as part of your recovery journey. (You can always add more later, but start small for now.)

2) Go through your social media accounts and review to what extent your social feeds are helping or hindering your recovery. Which accounts or types of posts tend to prompt negative emotions in you? And, conversely, which make you feel better? Consider unfollowing or muting potentially problematic accounts for the next thirty days and see if you miss them. You can always un-mute or re-follow later.

3) Work through the questions and exercises in the section on re-discovering your non-food interests and commit to one activity you are going to be trying out for the next month. Make sure you capture your commitment in writing in your recovery journal.

4) Revisit the first section in this chapter and use the guidelines there to start defining dedicated blocks of food thinking time that you'll use specifically to reflect on your binge eating recovery. Make sure you set a clear agenda for each block and capture it in your recovery journal.

PART THREE:
WORKSHEETS

HOW TO USE THE WORKSHEETS

Now that we've gone through the five pillars of recovery, and you've committed to spending a full year on getting better, the next step is to put your new-found knowledge into action. The following section will give you **sixteen worksheets and trackers** to help support you in that process, building on the exercises you've already encountered in the previous chapters.

Each of the worksheets comes with its own instructions. I highly recommend that you get the **free, printable versions** from www.bingeeatingrecoveryproject.com/worksheets. You will find those much more convenient than writing directly in this book. When visiting www.bingeeatingrecoveryproject.com/worksheets, you'll be asked to enter a password in order to access the downloads. Your password is:

ReaderBonus260848

If downloading the worksheets is not an option for you, you can also keep track of your answers by noting down the question number and relevant answer in your journal (e.g. Q6c, Q7e).

Key Principles

Before you get started with the actual worksheets, there are a few general considerations and preparations worth bearing in mind, especially for the self-reflection questionnaires and exercises:

- **Don't complete all the worksheets at once.** The idea is that you take time to reflect; rushing through the exercises defeats the purpose. You may also end up feeling overwhelmed.

- **Set aside some alone time.** To explore your thoughts and feelings, you need time and space to think — and you need to be undisturbed. If you can't be sure you won't be interrupted at home, consider going to a park, library or coffee shop, and complete the worksheets there.

- **Have a journal or notebook ready.** Write down any observations you have from working through the worksheets or further questions you want to explore. If you are going out, take two pens just in case. I have been in situations where my pen ran out while I was in a coffee shop, and it's incredibly annoying.

- **There are no wrong answers.** A worksheet is not a test. You are not being scored and no one will see your answers except you. You're doing this purely to gain a better understanding of yourself and your binge eating. As long as you're giving it your best shot, you are doing exactly what's required of you.

- **You don't have to answer everything.** Your goal should be to complete the worksheets in full, but if you cannot answer a certain question despite your best efforts, it's time to move on. Don't spend lots of time agonising over it. As long as you are honouring the spirit of the exercise — which means you are challenging yourself and not just skipping questions that are hard or uncomfortable — it's fine to not answer a question or two. You can always return to them at a later point, if need be.

- **You may feel overwhelmed or triggered.** Self-reflection can flush out all sorts of difficult emotions you normally keep under lock and key. Go into these exercises with your eyes open. If you think you might end up feeling overwhelmed, be extra careful about not doing too many worksheets at once, and make sure you talk to someone.

- **It's okay to read through the questions in advance.** When doing self-reflection, there is some value in answering the questions spontaneously, without having thought about them beforehand, but if there is a chance they could be triggering or upsetting to you, it's probably best not to find out when you're at the library or the coffee shop. It is therefore absolutely fine for you to read through the worksheets in advance, if that makes you feel more comfortable.

- **Schedule a re-take for three months' time.** As you work through your recovery, your feelings and attitudes towards binge eating are likely to change. It's useful to re-take the worksheets periodically to make sure you stay in touch with your emotions around binge eating and have an up-to-date understanding of yourself as a binge eater. I would advise against anything more regular than once every three months, so you don't run the risk of over-analysis.

YOUR BINGE PROFILE

The goal of this worksheet is to capture key facts and metrics about your binge eating. This will help you to better understand yourself as a binge eater and face up to the scale of your binge eating problem.

If you are about to start working with a therapist or coach, or plan to open up to a friend or relative, you may also find it easier to describe your binge eating to them after you have worked through the questions in this profile.

Complete the questions as best as you can. Don't worry if you aren't 100% sure about a question or can't remember exact dates or figures.

PART 1: THE BASICS

What year did you first start binging?   _____

How old were you at the time?   _____

What do you remember about your early binging days?
(Write down as many details as possible, including locations, binge foods, triggers etc.)

_____

_____

_____

_____

_____

_____

_____

In total, how many years and months have you been binging now?   _____ Years _____ Months

On average, how many times do you binge a week? (Just give your best estimate here.)   _____

How many times do you binge in an average month? (Again, your best estimate will do.)   _____

In the past month, would you say your binging has been...?
☐ Much better than usual
☐ Slightly better than usual
☐ The same
☐ Slightly worse than usual
☐ Much worse than usual

YOUR BINGE PROFILE

If you feel your binging has been getting better or worse, what do you think is causing this?
(Write down as much detail as you can.)

_____

_____

Have you ever done any of the following after a binge?

- ☐ Tried to make yourself vomit
- ☐ Actually made yourself vomit
- ☐ Taken laxatives
- ☐ Exercised excessively to 'make up' for a binge
- ☐ Gone on a detox or 'cleanse'
- ☐ Fasted
- ☐ Skipped a meal or meals
- ☐ Other (specify) _____

In the past month, have you done any of the following after a binge?

- ☐ Tried to make yourself vomit
- ☐ Actually made yourself vomit
- ☐ Taken laxatives
- ☐ Exercised excessively to 'make up' for a binge
- ☐ Gone on a detox or 'cleanse'
- ☐ Fasted
- ☐ Skipped a meal or meals
- ☐ Other (specify) _____

Have you ever suffered from any other eating-related disorder?

- ☐ No
- ☐ Yes – anorexia
- ☐ Yes – bulimia
- ☐ Yes – other (specify) _____

How long do you think it will take you to recover from binge eating?

- ☐ Less than six months
- ☐ Six months to a year
- ☐ 1-2 years
- ☐ 3-5 years
- ☐ 5-10 years
- ☐ More than 10 years
- ☐ (I don't think I'll ever recover)

YOUR BINGE PROFILE

Which of these have you ever tried for your binge eating?

- ☐ Self-help book
- ☐ Therapist (face-to-face)
- ☐ Therapist (telephone)
- ☐ Therapist (online)
- ☐ Group therapy
- ☐ Support group (face-to-face)
- ☐ Support group (online)
- ☐ Online chats/forums
- ☐ Life coach
- ☐ Other type of coach/counsellor

And which have you used in the past month?

- ☐ Self-help book
- ☐ Therapist (face-to-face)
- ☐ Therapist (telephone)
- ☐ Therapist (online)
- ☐ Group therapy
- ☐ Support group (face-to-face)
- ☐ Support group (online)
- ☐ Online chats/forums
- ☐ Life coach
- ☐ Other type of coach/counsellor

Which one of these have you found most helpful?

- ☐ Self-help book
- ☐ Therapist (face-to-face)
- ☐ Therapist (telephone)
- ☐ Therapist (online)
- ☐ Group therapy
- ☐ Support group (face-to-face)
- ☐ Support group (online)
- ☐ Online chats/forums
- ☐ Life coach
- ☐ Other type of coach/counsellor
- ☐ None
- ☐ Not sure

YOUR BINGE PROFILE

PART 2: PHYSICAL HEALTH

Which of the following have you ever experienced in connection with your binge eating?

- [ ] Stomach pains
- [ ] Extreme fullness/feeling you might burst
- [ ] Constipation
- [ ] Diarrhoea
- [ ] Mucus/slime in your bowel movements
- [ ] Heartburn
- [ ] General indigestion
- [ ] Vomiting (not deliberate)
- [ ] Racing heart
- [ ] Sweating
- [ ] Shortness of breath
- [ ] Sudden tiredness/desire to sleep
- [ ] Passing out
- [ ] Swollen tongue
- [ ] Bad skin/breakouts
- [ ] Dry skin
- [ ] Other (specify) _____

And which of these have you experienced in the past month?

- [ ] Stomach pains
- [ ] Extreme fullness/feeling you might burst
- [ ] Constipation
- [ ] Diarrhoea
- [ ] Mucus/slime in your bowel movements
- [ ] Heartburn
- [ ] General indigestion
- [ ] Vomiting (not deliberate)
- [ ] Racing heart
- [ ] Sweating
- [ ] Shortness of breath
- [ ] Sudden tiredness/desire to sleep
- [ ] Passing out
- [ ] Swollen tongue
- [ ] Bad skin/breakouts
- [ ] Dry skin
- [ ] Other (specify) _____

YOUR BINGE PROFILE

Which one of the following statements best describes you?

☐ My physical health has already suffered because of my binges

☐ My health has suffered a bit, but nothing permanent

☐ My health has probably suffered, but I'm not overly concerned

☐ I don't think my binges have had any impact on my physical health so far

And which one of these best describes you?

☐ I am increasingly worried about the physical damage my binges are causing

☐ I am getting a little more worried

☐ I am getting a little less worried

☐ I am increasingly less worried about the physical damage of my binges

☐ My level of concern hasn't really changed

Have you spoken to a doctor, nurse or other medical professional about any of the physical side effects of binge eating?

☐ Yes

☐ No

If you haven't yet spoken to a medical professional about the physical side effects of your binge eating, what would convince you to do so?

☐ If my binges got worse/my physical health suffered more

☐ If I suddenly started experiencing new physical side effects

☐ If a partner/friend/family member asked me to

☐ If I had a better/more understanding doctor

☐ Not sure – just hadn't occurred to me

☐ Nothing

Which one of the following statements best describes how much you know about binge eating and its effect on physical health?

☐ I am very well informed

☐ I am fairly well informed, but there are some things I'm not sure about

☐ I thought I was well informed, but I'm starting to realise there are gaps in my knowledge

☐ I have fairly limited knowledge about the physical side effects of binge eating

☐ I know virtually nothing about how binge eating affects physical health

And which of these statements best describes you?

☐ I recognise I don't care as much about the impact on my physical health as I should

☐ I should probably care more, but I have bigger problems to deal with first

☐ I already care a lot about the impact on my physical health

☐ I don't think I have anything to worry about as far as physical health is concerned

YOUR BINGE PROFILE

PART 3: MENTAL HEALTH

Which of the following statements about your overall mental health do you agree with?

☐ It's much better than it used to be

☐ It's slightly better than it used to be

☐ It's pretty much the same

☐ It's slightly worse than it used to be

☐ It's much worse than it used to be

And which of these best describes you?

☐ I understand binge eating can be a serious mental health condition and I am conscious of the effects it's having on my own mental health

☐ I understand it's seen as a mental health condition, but in my case it's just about food

☐ I didn't realise binge eating was considered a mental health condition

Which of the following do you agree with?

☐ Binge eating has had a severely negative impact on my mental health

☐ Binge eating has had a somewhat negative impact

☐ Binge eating has had no impact on my mental health

Have you ever felt any of the following in connection with your binge eating?

☐ Depressed

☐ Anxious

☐ Ashamed

☐ Isolated from others

☐ Hopeless

☐ Unable to connect with others on a meaningful level

☐ Suicidal

☐ Other (specify) _____

In the past month, have you felt any of the following in connection with your binge eating?

☐ Depressed

☐ Anxious

☐ Ashamed

☐ Isolated from others

☐ Hopeless

☐ Unable to connect with others on a meaningful level

☐ Suicidal

☐ Other (specify) _____

YOUR BINGE PROFILE

IF YOU ANSWERED YES TO ANY: Have you ever sought advice from a medical or mental health professional about this?

- ☐ Yes
- ☐ No

If you haven't yet spoken to a professional, what would make you consider doing so?

- ☐ If things got worse/I felt really bad
- ☐ If I suddenly started experiencing mental health issues I hadn't had before
- ☐ If my doctor was better/more understanding
- ☐ If I could get access to or afford seeing a mental health professional
- ☐ Not sure - just hadn't occurred to me
- ☐ Nothing

Have you ever been diagnosed as suffering from any of the following?

- ☐ Depression
- ☐ Anxiety disorder
- ☐ Panic attacks
- ☐ Bipolar disorder
- ☐ Other (specify) _____

IMPORTANT: If you are feeling hopeless, depressed and/or suicidal, whether about your binge eating or anything else, speak to your doctor or a mental health professional as soon as possible. There is lots of help available – don't delay asking for it.

YOUR BINGE PROFILE

PART 4: SOCIAL AND PRIVATE LIFE

Have you ever done any of the following because of your binge eating?

☐ Cancelled an appointment or date with a friend, partner or family member
☐ Lied or made up excuses to get out of social commitments
☐ Pretended you're not home
☐ Pretended you're sick
☐ Hidden food from other people
☐ Avoided sex or intimacy with a partner
☐ Failed to show up at big life events (e.g. birthdays, weddings, funerals)
☐ Refused to go out for dinner or eat in front of other people
☐ Refused to have your photograph taken
☐ Refused to take part in an activity (e.g. going swimming)
☐ Other (specify) _____

In the past month, have you done any of the following because of your binge eating?

☐ Cancelled an appointment or date with a friend, partner or family member
☐ Lied or made up excuses to get out of social commitments
☐ Pretended you're not home
☐ Pretended you're sick
☐ Hidden food from other people
☐ Avoided sex or intimacy with a partner
☐ Failed to show up at big life events (e.g. birthdays, weddings, funerals)
☐ Refused to go out for dinner or eat in front of other people
☐ Refused to have your photograph taken
☐ Refused to take part in an activity (e.g. going swimming)
☐ Other (specify) _____

Which of the following statements best describes you?

☐ My binge has a had a big negative impact on my social and private life
☐ It's had some impact
☐ I don't let my binge eating affect my social and private life

Would you say the impact your binge eating is having on your social and private life is getting...?

☐ Much worse
☐ A little worse
☐ A little better
☐ Much better
☐ Stayed roughly the same

YOUR BINGE PROFILE

Thinking about how your binge eating affects other people in your life, would you say you are...?

☐ Very worried about the impact your binge eating is having on them
☐ Slightly worried
☐ Not worried at all

If you are worried about the impact on others, what exactly are you concerned about?

_____

_____

_____

_____

Who knows that you have a binge eating problem?

☐ Partner
☐ Parent(s)
☐ Child(ren)
☐ Other family member(s)
☐ Friend(s)
☐ Colleague(s)
☐ Doctor or other medical professional
☐ Other (specify) _____

Which of these statements do you agree with?

☐ I plan to open up to more people about my binge eating
☐ I'd like to open up but I don't know how to
☐ I'm too embarrassed/ashamed to open up
☐ I don't see the point in bothering other people with this
☐ Other people wouldn't know how to help me anyway

YOUR BINGE PROFILE

PART 5: FINANCES

For the following questions, estimate the figures as best you can.

On average, how much do you spend when you buy food to binge on?   _____

How much money do you spend on binge food per week?   _____

Based on these estimates, how much do you spend a month?   _____

Look back at the questions in Part 1 and the number of years and months you said you have been binging. Based on this and your average weekly and monthly binge spend, calculate how much money you have spent on binge food throughout your lifetime.

For example, if you spend an average of £25 a week on binge food and have been binging for three years and four months, your calculation would look as follows:

£25 x 4 = monthly binge spend of £100
£25 x 52 = annual binge spend of £1,300
Annual spend of £1,300 x 3 = £3,900 over three years
Monthly spend of £100 x 4 = £400 over four months
Total: £4,300 total lifetime binge spend

So far in my life, I have spent roughly _____ on binge food.

How do you feel about the lifetime spend you have just calculated?
- [ ] It's much more than I thought
- [ ] It's a little more than I thought
- [ ] It's a little less than I thought
- [ ] It's much less than I thought
- [ ] It's roughly in line with what I thought
- [ ] I had never thought about my binge spend before

Have you ever done any of the following?
- [ ] Gone into debt or your overdraft to be able to buy food
- [ ] Borrowed money to buy food
- [ ] Stolen money from others to buy food
- [ ] Stolen food from others
- [ ] Delayed or cancelled other purchases in order to buy food
- [ ] Missed out on holidays or other fun things because your money had already gone on food

YOUR BINGE PROFILE

In the past month, have you done any of the following?

☐ Gone into debt or your overdraft to be able to buy food

☐ Borrowed money to buy food

☐ Stolen money from others to buy food

☐ Stolen food from others

☐ Delayed or cancelled other purchases in order to buy food

☐ Missed out on holidays or other fun things because your money had already gone on food

Which of these statements do you agree with?

☐ I would have a much better lifestyle today if I hadn't spent so much on food over the years

☐ I would have rather spent that money on other things, but I don't think I missed out too much

☐ I don't really spend that much despite my binges, so the impact is minimal

☐ I spend a lot on food but I can afford it, so I'm not too worried

PART 6: REFLECTION

How do you feel having completed this questionnaire?

☐ It's made me realise my binge eating is much worse than I thought

☐ It's made me realise it's a little worse than I thought

☐ It's largely confirmed what I already knew

☐ It's made me realise my binge eating actually isn't as bad as I'd feared

How do you feel about your recovery prospects now?

☐ I am much more confident that I'll be able to recover

☐ I am a little less confident about my recovery than I was before

☐ I am much less confident about being able to recover now

Based on the new insight you gained into your binge eating patterns and behaviours, what one step will you take today to help you towards recovery?

_____

_____

_____

_____

THE BINGE EATING RECOVERY PROJECT

YOUR ARCHETYPAL BINGE

Your Archetypal Binge is your most common binge pattern. Identifying your Archetypal Binge will help you focus your recovery efforts and prevention tactics on where it matters most.

We will start by reviewing your binge patterns over the past week.

Q1. In the past week, how many times have you binged? (Count each binge separately. If you binged twice on the same day, count this as two binges.) _____

Q2. Still thinking about the past week specifically, how many times did you binge on each of these days?
(If you didn't binge on a day, put zero.)

Monday   _____
Tuesday   _____
Wednesday   _____
Thursday   _____
Friday   _____
Saturday   _____
Sunday   _____

Q3. And how many times did you binge at the following times of day in the past week? (If you didn't binge at a particular time, put zero.)

6-8am   _____
8-10am   _____
10-12pm   _____
12-2pm   _____
2-4pm   _____
4-6pm   _____
6-8pm   _____
8-10pm   _____
10pm-midnight   _____
After midnight   _____

Q4. In the past week, how many times did you binge in the following locations? (If you didn't binge in a particular location, put zero.)

At home   _____
At work   _____
In my car   _____
On public transport (eg bus, train, etc.)   _____
While walking   _____
Other (specify)   _____   _____

YOUR ARCHETYPAL BINGE

Q5. And how many times did you binge under the following circumstances in the past week? (Again, put zero for anything that doesn't apply.)

When I was alone _____

When I was with other people _____

On the way to work _____

On the way back from work _____

After I dropped off my kids at school/nursery _____

After my kids got back from school/nursery _____

After a long day _____

After a conflict or confrontation with another person _____

When I was bored _____

When I had too much to do _____

Other (specify) _____ _____

Q6. Still looking at your binging in the past week and thinking about when, where and how you binged, would you say...

☐ This was a fairly average week of binging for me (SKIP TO Q7)

☐ I usually binge on different days or times of day (GO TO Q6a)

Q6a. On which days would you normally binge?

☐ Monday

☐ Tuesday

☐ Wednesday

☐ Thursday

☐ Friday

☐ Saturday

☐ Sunday

Q6b. And which times of day?

☐ 6–8am

☐ 8–10am

☐ 10–12pm

☐ 12–2pm

☐ 2–4pm

☐ 4–6pm

☐ 6–8pm

☐ 8–10pm

☐ 10pm–midnight

☐ After midnight

YOUR ARCHETYPAL BINGE

Q6c. And in which locations?

- [ ] At home
- [ ] At work
- [ ] In my car
- [ ] On public transport (eg bus, train, metro etc.)
- [ ] While walking
- [ ] Other (specify) _____

Q6d. And under which circumstances?

- [ ] When I am alone
- [ ] When I am with other people
- [ ] On the way to work
- [ ] On the way back from work
- [ ] After I drop off my kids at school/nursery
- [ ] After my kids get back from school/nursery
- [ ] After a long day
- [ ] After a conflict or confrontation with another person
- [ ] When I am bored
- [ ] When I have too much to do
- [ ] Other (specify) _____

Now carefully review your answers in the previous section and answer the following questions as best as you can.

Q7. On average, I binge _____ times a week and _____ times a month.

Q8. The day(s) when most of my binges happen is/are... _____

Q9. The time(s) of day when most of my binges happen is/are... _____

Q10. The location(s) where most of my binges happen is/are... _____

_____

_____

Q11. The circumstances around most of my binges are... _____

_____

_____

YOUR ARCHETYPAL BINGE

Q12. Based on your answers, now try to describe your most common binge pattern or Archetypal Binge.
Go into as much detail as possible. Include specific locations. times of day and what you are doing at the time.

An example might be: 'My Archetypal Binge takes place on a Wednesday or Thursday. when I am getting off the train after work and instead of walking straight home I take a detour and stop off at the shops.'

Remember. you are not trying to describe what all your binges look like. This is about describing your binge eating in its most typical form.

My Archetypal Binge is as follows:

_____

_____

_____

_____

_____

_____

_____

_____

_____

_____

_____

_____

_____

_____

_____

_____

_____

_____

REVERSE-ENGINEERING

The purpose of this exercise is to help you understand what goes right when you're having a good day with your binge eating — and what you can do to make those good days happen more often. Important: A 'good day' doesn't necessarily have to mean a binge-free day. It's any day that you perceive to be better than average.

PART 1: FINISH THE SENTENCE

Q1. Complete the following sentences as best as you can.

The last time I had a good day was... _____

_____

What made that day good was... _____

_____

What my good days have in common is... _____

_____

The reason I don't have more good days is... _____

_____

The biggest step I could take towards having more good days is... _____

_____

PART 2: AGREE OR DISAGREE

Q2. Rate the following statements on a scale of 1 to 5. 1 = disagree strongly and 5= agree strongly

On a good day, I keep busy and don't have lots of unstructured time during the day.	①	②	③	④	⑤
On a good day, I don't have to stick to a schedule.	①	②	③	④	⑤
On a good day, I don't have to go to work.	①	②	③	④	⑤
On a good day, I keep to my usual routine.	①	②	③	④	⑤
On a good day, I deliberately shake up my usual routine.	①	②	③	④	⑤
On a good day, I look after myself.	①	②	③	④	⑤
On a good day, I move my body or exercise.	①	②	③	④	⑤
On a good day, I make time for meditation or mindfulness exercises.	①	②	③	④	⑤
On a good day, my clothes are neat and clean.	①	②	③	④	⑤
On a good day, I wear clothes that fit me and don't make me feel restricted.	①	②	③	④	⑤
On a good day, I like the clothes I am wearing.	①	②	③	④	⑤
On a good day, I shower and wash my hair.	①	②	③	④	⑤
On a good day, I take care doing my makeup or nails.	①	②	③	④	⑤
On a good day, I make a point of being nice to myself.	①	②	③	④	⑤
On a good day, I don't worry about what I wear or how I look.	①	②	③	④	⑤
On a good day, I stop negative thoughts as soon as they arise.	①	②	③	④	⑤

REVERSE-ENGINEERING

On a good day, I make a point of being nice to others.	① ② ③ ④ ⑤
On a good day, I am not alone.	① ② ③ ④ ⑤
On a good day, I talk to someone if I feel a binge could be coming.	① ② ③ ④ ⑤
On a good day, I spend quality time with my partner.	① ② ③ ④ ⑤
On a good day, I spend quality time with my children.	① ② ③ ④ ⑤
On a good day, I spend quality time with friends.	① ② ③ ④ ⑤
On a good day, I spend quality time on my own.	① ② ③ ④ ⑤
On a good day, my house is tidy and clean.	① ② ③ ④ ⑤
On a good day, I don't weigh myself.	① ② ③ ④ ⑤
On a good day, I am so busy I don't even think about food.	① ② ③ ④ ⑤
On a good day, someone else takes care of the cooking.	① ② ③ ④ ⑤
On a good day, I don't spend time in front of the mirror.	① ② ③ ④ ⑤
On a good day, I don't go shopping/to the stores.	① ② ③ ④ ⑤
On a good day, I make time to read.	① ② ③ ④ ⑤
On a good day, I don't spend much time on my phone.	① ② ③ ④ ⑤
On a good day, I make time to do something I truly love.	① ② ③ ④ ⑤
On a good day, I write in my journal.	① ② ③ ④ ⑤
On a good day, I have planned exactly what I am going to eat and stick with it.	① ② ③ ④ ⑤
On a good day, I just allow myself to eat and don't worry about it.	① ② ③ ④ ⑤
On a good day, I walk away from conversations about food or bodyweight.	① ② ③ ④ ⑤
On a good day, I limit my use of social media.	① ② ③ ④ ⑤

PART 3: TAKING ACTION

Q3. Look through your answers to the previous exercise and pick out five statements that you scored 4 or 5 and write them down. (If you don't have five, just take however many you have.)

1. On a good day, … _____
2. On a good day, … _____
3. On a good day, … _____
4. On a good day, … _____
5. On a good day, … _____

Q4. Now pick one of these statements and brainstorm ideas for how you can make this happen at least once over the next week. Be as precise and as detailed as possible.

Statement: On a good day, _____

_____

_____

REVERSE-ENGINEERING

What I will do to make this happen over the next week: _____

_____

_____

_____

_____

_____

_____

_____

_____

_____

_____

PART 4: REVIEW

In a week's time, return to this sheet and review what impact the exercise has had by answering the following questions.

Q5. Overall, did you feel this exercise has been helpful? _____

_____

Q6. What could you change to make it more helpful? _____

_____

Q7. Will you try to keep it as part of your recovery routine? _____

_____

Q8. Is there another statement you want to try out instead? _____

_____

BINGE EATING QUESTIONNAIRE

The purpose of this questionnaire is self-reflection. It will prompt you to explore how you really feel about your binge eating problem, its causes and triggers, and your prospect of recovery. You will be presented with a list of 150 statements about binge eating and asked how much you agree with each of them on a scale of 1 to 5. 1 = disagree completely and 5 = agree completely.

There is no scoring system. You won't get a diagnosis at the end or an assessment of how bad your binge eating is. The goal is simply to prompt you to think about your binge eating in new, deeper ways. Keep a record of your answers and re-take the questionnaire periodically to track how your attitudes and emotions change over time.

Deep down, I have stopped believing I'll ever get better   ① ② ③ ④ ⑤

If I keep trying, I will eventually figure out how to stop binging   ① ② ③ ④ ⑤

I wish I had more support in fighting this   ① ② ③ ④ ⑤

I know I should talk to someone about my binge eating, but I don't know what to say   ① ② ③ ④ ⑤

I don't have enough money to get the help I need   ① ② ③ ④ ⑤

I wish I had never, ever gone on a diet   ① ② ③ ④ ⑤

I worry I am passing my disordered eating on to my children   ① ② ③ ④ ⑤

I am a bad role model to my children because of my binge eating   ① ② ③ ④ ⑤

Binge eating is stopping me from forming relationships and connecting with others   ① ② ③ ④ ⑤

There is no rhyme or reason to my binges — they are completely random   ① ② ③ ④ ⑤

My binges are highly predictable. There is a clear pattern   ① ② ③ ④ ⑤

When the urge to binge hits me, I feel completely out of control   ① ② ③ ④ ⑤

When I binge, it feels like I am on autopilot   ① ② ③ ④ ⑤

If I wasn't a binge eater, I don't think I'd be with my current partner   ① ② ③ ④ ⑤

If I wasn't a binge eater, I'd have a better career   ① ② ③ ④ ⑤

If I wasn't a binge eater, I'd have more money   ① ② ③ ④ ⑤

If I wasn't a binge eater, my life would be so much better   ① ② ③ ④ ⑤

If I wasn't a binge eater, I'd stand up for myself more   ① ② ③ ④ ⑤

Most people with a binge eating problem eventually get better   ① ② ③ ④ ⑤

Once a binge eater, always a binge eater   ① ② ③ ④ ⑤

My biggest fear is that other people might find out about my binge eating   ① ② ③ ④ ⑤

If people knew I had a binge eating problem, they'd lose respect for me   ① ② ③ ④ ⑤

If people knew I had a binge eating problem, they'd make fun of me behind my back   ① ② ③ ④ ⑤

If people knew I had a binge eating problem, they would try to help me   ① ② ③ ④ ⑤

Binge eaters are pretty pathetic, and I hate that I am one of them   ① ② ③ ④ ⑤

I have a particularly severe form of binge eating   ① ② ③ ④ ⑤

I have a relatively mild form of binge eating   ① ② ③ ④ ⑤

I would find it helpful to talk to other people with binge eating problems   ① ② ③ ④ ⑤

Most people who know me know I have a binge eating problem   ① ② ③ ④ ⑤

BINGE EATING QUESTIONNAIRE

Not talking about your binge eating only makes the problem worse	① ② ③ ④ ⑤
I wish I had opened up to other people sooner	① ② ③ ④ ⑤
I have spent truly staggering amounts of money on my binges	① ② ③ ④ ⑤
Restrictive dieting is the biggest reason I'm a binge eater today	① ② ③ ④ ⑤
I think I have a genetic predisposition towards binge eating	① ② ③ ④ ⑤
Most of my family is screwed up about food, so it's no surprise I binge	① ② ③ ④ ⑤
If my parents had taught me better eating habits when I was growing up, I wouldn't be a binge eater today	① ② ③ ④ ⑤
Everyone else in my family is normal around food, so I don't know why I ended up being like this	① ② ③ ④ ⑤
My parents would blame themselves if I told them about my binge eating	① ② ③ ④ ⑤
I wish people took binge eating more seriously	① ② ③ ④ ⑤
I worry other people don't think binge eating is a serious problem	① ② ③ ④ ⑤
I don't believe binge eating is a real eating disorder	① ② ③ ④ ⑤
Binge eating is not as serious as anorexia or bulimia	① ② ③ ④ ⑤
Calling binge eating an eating disorder is just a way to make fat people feel better about themselves	① ② ③ ④ ⑤
I'm not calling my binges an eating disorder because I don't want to make excuses for myself	① ② ③ ④ ⑤
At the end of the day, the solution to binge eating is better self-discipline	① ② ③ ④ ⑤
I don't have enough willpower to stop binge eating	① ② ③ ④ ⑤
Sometimes I actually enjoy my binges	① ② ③ ④ ⑤
When I finally give in to the urge to binge, it's such a relief	① ② ③ ④ ⑤
I often plan my binges meticulously and look forward to them	① ② ③ ④ ⑤
My binges are the only time I allow myself to eat the food I really want	① ② ③ ④ ⑤
I don't even know which foods I like anymore	① ② ③ ④ ⑤
I can't eat anything without feeling guilty	① ② ③ ④ ⑤
I can't go anywhere without people commenting on my weight or food choices	① ② ③ ④ ⑤
I hate it when people at work ask me what I'm having for lunch	① ② ③ ④ ⑤
Everybody is talking so much about food all the time	① ② ③ ④ ⑤
When someone says they need to lose weight, it makes me feel awful	① ② ③ ④ ⑤
I have lost all sense of what normal eating behaviour looks like	① ② ③ ④ ⑤
I just want someone to tell me exactly what to eat and when	① ② ③ ④ ⑤
Socialising and spending time with others has become harder because of my binge eating	① ② ③ ④ ⑤
If people who knew me in high school/at university could see me now, they'd be shocked	① ② ③ ④ ⑤
I will never be able to accept my body at the weight it is now	① ② ③ ④ ⑤
I know people say you have to stop dieting to recover from binge eating, but I'm just not willing to accept that	① ② ③ ④ ⑤

BINGE EATING QUESTIONNAIRE

I have stopped dieting and the binges are still happening, so now I don't know what to think ① ② ③ ④ ⑤

The longer I've had this problem, the less I feel I understand it ① ② ③ ④ ⑤

I am starting to get a better understanding of my binge eating ① ② ③ ④ ⑤

Sugar is my biggest problem and I must find a way to cut it out of my diet ① ② ③ ④ ⑤

Processed foods are my biggest problem and I must find a way to cut them out of my diet ① ② ③ ④ ⑤

Carbs are my biggest problem and I must find a way to cut them out of my diet ① ② ③ ④ ⑤

Blaming processed foods, carbs or sugar for binges is simplistic and goes against the best available scientific evidence ① ② ③ ④ ⑤

I am making a point of educating myself on binge eating and its causes ① ② ③ ④ ⑤

I actually have very little idea of what the latest scientific thinking on binge eating is ① ② ③ ④ ⑤

I am too quick to believe what other people tell me about how to fix my binge eating ① ② ③ ④ ⑤

I don't really know who to trust when it comes to binge eating advice ① ② ③ ④ ⑤

I think the food industry is largely to blame for people's binge eating problems ① ② ③ ④ ⑤

The medical establishment is not being honest about the causes of binge eating ① ② ③ ④ ⑤

The real reason why people binge eat is being kept from the public ① ② ③ ④ ⑤

Professional qualifications aren't really that important when it comes to giving binge eating advice; it's all about life experience ① ② ③ ④ ⑤

I would rather seek binge eating advice from an alternative or complementary practitioner than a medical doctor ① ② ③ ④ ⑤

It's helpful that concepts like body positivity are being talked about more ① ② ③ ④ ⑤

I have no idea how body positivity is meant to apply to me ① ② ③ ④ ⑤

Medical school teaches doctors nothing about diet, nutrition or eating problems like mine ① ② ③ ④ ⑤

I accept I can't diet or restrict calories while I'm trying to recover ① ② ③ ④ ⑤

If I end up putting on weight during my recovery, so be it ① ② ③ ④ ⑤

If I can't lose weight, there's no point even trying to recover ① ② ③ ④ ⑤

No recovery method that actually works will make you put on weight ① ② ③ ④ ⑤

I feel like I am finally starting to make peace with my body ① ② ③ ④ ⑤

No one who looks like me can reasonably be expected to be happy ① ② ③ ④ ⑤

The way I look is the biggest reason I am not achieving what I want in life ① ② ③ ④ ⑤

I know I have a tendency to put far too much importance on the way I look and what I weigh ① ② ③ ④ ⑤

I am getting better at not judging myself too harshly ① ② ③ ④ ⑤

There are lots of recovery methods and programmes I haven't tried yet ① ② ③ ④ ⑤

I am too trusting when it comes to binge eating advice and end up disappointed when things don't work out for me ① ② ③ ④ ⑤

I think I am quite vulnerable to scams and snake oil merchants ① ② ③ ④ ⑤

BINGE EATING QUESTIONNAIRE

There is lots of poor advice about binge eating out there, but I know how to tell good
advice from bad   ① ② ③ ④ ⑤

Awareness and understanding of binge eating is improving all the time, and this
makes me hopeful for my chances of recovery   ① ② ③ ④ ⑤

There is much more support available for binge eaters today than when I first
started binging   ① ② ③ ④ ⑤

There is probably much more support and help available than I realise   ① ② ③ ④ ⑤

Hearing binge eating referred to as an 'eating disorder' makes me cringe   ① ② ③ ④ ⑤

I am excited about trying out different recovery methods to see what might work for
me   ① ② ③ ④ ⑤

Trial and error is part of the recovery process   ① ② ③ ④ ⑤

Progress beats perfection when it comes to binge eating   ① ② ③ ④ ⑤

I know everyone says 'progress beats perfection', but I don't buy into that. You either
stop binging completely, or you've failed   ① ② ③ ④ ⑤

I may not ever be completely binge-free, but I can still get much better than I am today   ① ② ③ ④ ⑤

You have to accept yourself at the weight you are, or you'll never stop binging   ① ② ③ ④ ⑤

It makes me angry when people say I should accept my body as it is   ① ② ③ ④ ⑤

If I really could get better, it would have happened by now   ① ② ③ ④ ⑤

I am too old to change   ① ② ③ ④ ⑤

No one really understands or knows how to treat binge eating   ① ② ③ ④ ⑤

I'd like to try medication for my binge eating, but I don't have the guts to ask my
doctor for it   ① ② ③ ④ ⑤

I'd never consider going on medication for my binge eating   ① ② ③ ④ ⑤

Going on medication is probably the logical next step for me   ① ② ③ ④ ⑤

There is lots of controversy around using medication to treat binge eating, so I'll
leave it until more research has been done   ① ② ③ ④ ⑤

I don't want to talk my friends and family about my binges because they'll be worried   ① ② ③ ④ ⑤

I should probably be more careful about accepting binge eating advice from people
on the internet   ① ② ③ ④ ⑤

I wish everyone would just shut up about diets and losing weight   ① ② ③ ④ ⑤

I should spend less time on social media   ① ② ③ ④ ⑤

I feel worse about myself and my binge eating whenever I spend lots of time on
social media   ① ② ③ ④ ⑤

I think about food all the time   ① ② ③ ④ ⑤

I can't even remember what my interests were before I started binge eating   ① ② ③ ④ ⑤

I wish I had a hobby to distract me from food and binge eating   ① ② ③ ④ ⑤

There's no point exercising until I have my binge eating under control   ① ② ③ ④ ⑤

I feel better about myself when I move my body or exercise   ① ② ③ ④ ⑤

I would like to get into exercising and move my body more regularly   ① ② ③ ④ ⑤

I often have no idea what to do with myself in my spare time   ① ② ③ ④ ⑤

BINGE EATING QUESTIONNAIRE

I spend most of my life being bored	① ② ③ ④ ⑤
I spend too much of my time alone	① ② ③ ④ ⑤
I can't remember the last book I read	① ② ③ ④ ⑤
I would like to see a therapist about my binge eating	① ② ③ ④ ⑤
I haven't really looked into what therapy options might be available to me	① ② ③ ④ ⑤
I always say I'm going to change, but I never do	① ② ③ ④ ⑤
I know at the end of the day recovery is down to me	① ② ③ ④ ⑤
I find it hard to forgive myself after a setback	① ② ③ ④ ⑤
I feel guilty all the time	① ② ③ ④ ⑤
Binge eaters need discipline more than self-care	① ② ③ ④ ⑤
I'd love a self-care routine, but I have no idea where to start	① ② ③ ④ ⑤
Self-care feels a bit silly to me	① ② ③ ④ ⑤
There is no one to blame for my binge eating except me	① ② ③ ④ ⑤
I should be taking more responsibility for my binge eating	① ② ③ ④ ⑤
I am too quick to make excuses for my binge eating	① ② ③ ④ ⑤
I am learning to be more accountable for my own actions around food	① ② ③ ④ ⑤
There are lots of factors that play into binge eating. You can't just blame it all on yourself.	① ② ③ ④ ⑤
I find advice about binge eating confusing or contradictory	① ② ③ ④ ⑤
I am in a better position to recover today than I have been in a long time	① ② ③ ④ ⑤

UNDERSTANDING YOUR TRIGGERS

Triggers can play a big role in binge eating, but you may not always be fully aware of what yours are and how they interact with your binges. The following questions will help you build up your understanding of your own triggers as well as your emotions and attitudes towards them.

Keep a record of your answers and re-do this worksheet periodically, especially if you feel your binge behaviours are changing.

Q1. How important a role do you believe triggers play in your binge eating?

☐ Very important
☐ Slightly important
☐ Slightly unimportant
☐ Completely unimportant

Q2. How much do you know about your triggers?

☐ I know exactly what my triggers are
☐ I have some understanding of my triggers
☐ I know very little about my triggers
☐ I know virtually nothing about my triggers

Q3. Which of these statements do you agree with? (Select all that apply.)

☐ I feel embarrassed to talk about triggers
☐ Triggers are just an excuse to make people feel better about their lack of self-discipline
☐ I have discussed my triggers with other people
☐ Knowing what your triggers are is an important step towards recovery
☐ I worry that triggers are too simplistic an explanation for my binges
☐ I would like to have a better understanding of my own triggers
☐ My binges are too random for there to be common triggers
☐ Triggers are a self-fulfilling prophecy
☐ I feel I am starting to get a better handle on my triggers
☐ I don't know enough about triggers to have much of an opinion about them

Q4. And which of these describe how you feel about food as a trigger? (Select all that apply.)

☐ All binge eaters are triggered by food on some level
☐ The concept of trigger foods is a construct of the diet industry
☐ Food is a less important trigger than many people think
☐ Certain foods are inherently triggering because of their composition or the ingredients they contain
☐ Emotions and circumstances are more powerful triggers than food
☐ There is no such thing as a trigger food
☐ It's harmful for binge eaters to try to eliminate supposed trigger foods

UNDERSTANDING YOUR TRIGGERS

Q5. Do you ever experience any of the following as triggers?

- [ ] Stress
- [ ] Boredom
- [ ] Too much time on your hands
- [ ] Conflict with a partner, family member or friend
- [ ] Conflict at work
- [ ] Deadlines
- [ ] Weighing yourself and being heavier than you thought
- [ ] Weighing yourself and being lighter than you thought
- [ ] Going clothes shopping
- [ ] Finding you can no longer fit into certain clothes in your wardrobe
- [ ] Wearing clothes that don't fit/are too tight
- [ ] Having to eat in public
- [ ] Being invited out for a meal
- [ ] Someone commenting on your weight or appearance
- [ ] Grief
- [ ] Feeling sad or depressed
- [ ] Feeling anxious
- [ ] Feeling fat or unattractive
- [ ] Looking at yourself in the mirror
- [ ] Spending time on social media
- [ ] Having an unexpected change to your usual routine
- [ ] Having someone cancel an appointment or date with you
- [ ] Being in a certain location
- [ ] Eating a specific food
- [ ] Eating more than you had planned
- [ ] Eating something different to what you had planned

Q6. In the past month, have any of the following played a part in any of your binges?

- [ ] Stress
- [ ] Boredom
- [ ] Too much time on your hands
- [ ] Conflict with a partner, family member or friend
- [ ] Conflict at work
- [ ] Deadlines
- [ ] Weighing yourself and being heavier than you thought
- [ ] Weighing yourself and being lighter than you thought
- [ ] Going clothes shopping
- [ ] Finding you can no longer fit into certain clothes in your wardrobe
- [ ] Wearing clothes that don't fit/are too tight

UNDERSTANDING YOUR TRIGGERS

☐ Having to eat in public
☐ Being invited out for a meal
☐ Someone commenting on your weight or appearance
☐ Grief
☐ Feeling sad or depressed
☐ Feeling anxious
☐ Feeling fat or unattractive
☐ Looking at yourself in the mirror
☐ Spending time on social media
☐ Having an unexpected change to your usual routine
☐ Having someone cancel an appointment or date with you
☐ Being in a certain location
☐ Eating a specific food
☐ Eating more than you had planned
☐ Eating something different to what you had planned

Q7. What do you believe are your five most common triggers? (Don't worry if you can't think of five. Just write down as many as you can.)

Trigger 1: _____
Trigger 2: _____
Trigger 3: _____
Trigger 4: _____
Trigger 5: _____

Q8. Which of the following have you ever done?
☐ Kept a trigger journal or tracker
☐ Developed strategies to deal with specific triggers
☐ Made a point of avoiding certain triggering situations
☐ Talked to a doctor or mental health professional about your triggers
☐ Talked to a partner, friend or family member about your triggers

Q9. What is one positive step you can take today to better deal with your triggers? (Write down as much detail as possible.) _____

_____
_____
_____
_____

FINISH THE SENTENCE

Complete the following 25 sentences. Keep your answers short and to the point. Repeat the exercise periodically to see how your thinking evolves over time.

Deep down, I think I binge eat because... _____

_____

The biggest thing that would help me stop binge eating is.... _____

_____

The person I most wish I could talk to about my binge eating is... _____

_____

If anyone is going to judge me badly for my binge eating it's... _____

_____

The biggest reason my previous recovery attempts have failed is... _____

_____

I feel most ashamed about my binge eating when... _____

_____

The best thing I've ever done to tackle my binge eating is... _____

_____

The biggest obstacle that's stopping me from getting better is... _____

_____

I secretly think people with binge eating problems are... _____

_____

The idea of talking to someone about my binge eating makes me feel... _____

_____

My biggest fear about my binge eating is... _____

_____

My biggest regret about binge eating is... _____

_____

FINISH THE SENTENCE

My binge eating tends to get better when... _____
_____

My binge eating tends to get worse when... _____
_____

What no one understands about binge eating is... _____
_____

The worst moment I've ever experienced with binge eating was... _____
_____

The one thing I wish I could be honest about is... _____
_____

The way my body looks makes me feel... _____
_____

I wish I could eat in a way that's... _____
_____

The most important thing I've learned about binge eating is... _____
_____

If I could go back in time, the one thing I would tell my younger self is... ____
_____

I wish I could... _____
_____

I wish I didn't... _____
_____

I wish I knew... _____
_____

One positive step I could take today is... _____
_____

SETTING RECOVERY GOALS

This worksheet will help you to set process goals for your recovery. Important: Process goals are actions you are going to take, not the results you are hoping to achieve.

PART 1: GETTING INTO THE RECOVERY MINDSET

Q1. Think of a person recovering from binge eating and imagine what kinds of positive actions they would take during their recovery. Don't worry if these actions are something you personally would or could do right now. We're just brainstorming general ideas. Make sure every action you write down is positive and something a person can actively do as opposed to something to avoid.

Example: A person recovering from binge eating would...eat three meals a day.

A person recovering from binge eating would... _____

_____

A person recovering from binge eating would... _____

_____

A person recovering from binge eating would... _____

_____

A person recovering from binge eating would... _____

_____

A person recovering from binge eating would... _____

_____

Q2. Next are some more specific scenarios to think about. Complete each sentence by describing a positive action a person in recovery would do.

After getting up in the morning, a person in recovery would... _____

_____

At the weekend, when preparing for the week ahead, a person in recovery would... _____

_____

When faced with a triggering situation, a person in recovery would... _____

_____

SETTING RECOVERY GOALS

When experiencing high levels of stress at home or at work, a person in recovery would...

_____

_____

When out for dinner with friends or family, a person in recovery would...   _____

_____

When going grocery shopping, a person in recovery would...   _____

_____

When offered food or snacks at work or in social situations, a person in recovery would...

_____

_____

When at risk of losing motivation or faith in the recovery process, a person in recovery would...

_____

_____

When feeling overwhelmed, a person in recovery would...   _____

_____

When suffering a setback, a person in recovery would...   _____

_____

SETTING RECOVERY GOALS

PART 2: DEFINING PROCESS GOALS

Q3. Now it's time to apply this kind of thinking to your own recovery process. Complete the following sentences as best as you can.

During my recovery year, the biggest change to my daily routine I want to make is...

_____

_____

One small, meaningful everyday change I will make is... _____

_____

One new, positive food habit I want to build during my recovery year is... _____

_____

One new skill I want to learn during my recovery year is... _____

_____

One easy, positive change I could start making right now is... _____

_____

Q4. Based on these, try to think of five food-related actions as well as five non-food related ones that you will do during your recovery year. These are your process goals.

Remember to make them positive and specific, and start small. You can always become more ambitious as you go along. For now, your focus should be on small, positive actions.

Your 5 Food-Related Recovery Actions

1. During my recovery year, I will... _____

_____

2. During my recovery year, I will... _____

_____

3. During my recovery year, I will... _____

_____

SETTING RECOVERY GOALS

4. During my recovery year, I will... _____

_____

5. During my recovery year, I will... _____

_____

Your 5 Non-Food Recovery Actions

1. During my recovery year, I will... _____

_____

2. During my recovery year, I will... _____

_____

3. During my recovery year, I will... _____

_____

4. During my recovery year, I will... _____

_____

5. During my recovery year, I will... _____

_____

PART 3: REVIEWING YOUR PROCESS

You should review your progress against your recovery goals on a regular basis, and adjust them if necessary. This doesn't need to be a hugely involved process; just make time once a month to look back at how well you have stuck to your process goals and what you might need to adjust.

You can do this informally, in your recovery journal, or by using the structure suggested on the Monthly Recovery Review worksheet. For now, the next step is making sure you commit to your first review session by filling in the date below.

My first progress review date will be on...   _____ /   / _____

YOUR RECOVERY REWARDS

Recovery rewards are a useful tool for structuring your recovery year and giving you something to work towards and look forward to. Your rewards should reward you for sticking with your process goals, as opposed to achieving a specific outcome (e.g. weight loss or being binge-free). They should also be unrelated to food.

You should set at least one reward per month, though it's also worth considering rewards for bigger milestones (e.g. three months in or at the half-way mark).

STEP 1: GET SOME INSPIRATION

If you already know what rewards you want to set, you can skip this section and go straight to Step 2.

If you could do with a bit of inspiration, take a look through the following list of rewards categories. Ideally, your rewards should be from a variety of categories. Remember, you don't have to plan all of your rewards for the full year right this second. Just get the first quarter done and return at a later point, if need be.

LITTLE LUXURIES
- A new fragrance
- Nail polish
- A silk scarf
- A new pair of shoes
- A massage or spa treatment

TRAVEL
- A weekend away
- A holiday
- A day or night out

ADVENTURE
- Climb a mountain
- Go for a hike
- Go cycling

CULTURE
- Go to a gig
- Go see a musical or play
- Visit a gallery or exhibition
- Buy a new book

YOUR RECOVERY REWARDS

STEP 2: MATCH UP REWARDS AND GOALS

Write down your process goals as well as any other positive behaviours or recovery milestones that you want to reward yourself for, and decide over what period you need to stick to your process goals to get the reward. Then match up your process goals with an appropriate reward of your choice.

Keep your time frames pretty short at the beginning. You can always set more ambitions goals as you progress.

Here is an example:

Process goal: Wash my hair every night
Time frame: One month
Reward: A new fragrance

Your process goals

Process goal #1: _____
Time frame: _____
Reward: _____

Process goal #2 _____
Time frame: _____
Reward: _____

Process goal #3 _____
Time frame: _____
Reward: _____

Process goal #4 _____
Time frame: _____
Reward: _____

Process goal #5 _____
Time frame: _____
Reward: _____

YOUR RECOVERY REWARDS

Process goal #6: _____

Time frame: _____

Reward: _____

Process goal #7 _____

Time frame: _____

Reward: _____

Process goal #8 _____

Time frame: _____

Reward: _____

Process goal #9 _____

Time frame: _____

Reward: _____

Process goal #10 _____

Time frame: _____

Reward: _____

YOUR RECOVERY REWARDS

STEP 3: MARK RECOVERY MILESTONES

In addition to the process goal rewards you have just set, it's also worth celebrating key milestones during your recovery year with rewards. I suggest you set and review these on a quarterly basis rather than trying to commit to a whole year's worth of rewards right from the start.

Again, remember: You should reward yourself for having stuck with the process for a certain amount of time; don't be tempted to link these milestones rewards to certain outcomes (e.g. being binge-free).

To mark the first week of my recovery year, I will reward myself with...

_____

_____

When I've made it through the first month of my recovery year, I will reward myself with...

_____

_____

Two months down the line, I will reward myself with...

_____

_____

To mark the first quarter of my recovery year, the reward I will give myself is...

_____

_____

04

CHALLENGING FOOD DOGMA

Use this worksheet to develop a better understanding of your beliefs and value judgments around food, and to challenge food dogma during your recovery.

Q1. Which of these factors and characteristics matter to you when deciding which foods to buy and eat?

- [ ] Taste/flavour
- [ ] Texture
- [ ] Price/affordability
- [ ] A food I like
- [ ] A food my family likes
- [ ] Calorie content
- [ ] Macros (protein, fat or carb content/ratio)
- [ ] Micros (vitamins, minerals, antioxidants, fibre etc)
- [ ] Functional properties (e.g. helps digestion, boosts energy)
- [ ] General healthfulness
- [ ] Fits into my meal plan
- [ ] Fits into the diet I follow (e.g. paleo, low-carb)
- [ ] Familiarity — whether I've tried it before
- [ ] Novelty/innovation — whether it's something new
- [ ] Convenience — easy to prepare/eat
- [ ] Seen it online/on social media
- [ ] Used/endorsed by celebrities
- [ ] Something I have a recipe for
- [ ] Brand/manufacturer
- [ ] Level of processing
- [ ] Number of ingredients
- [ ] Clean labelling
- [ ] No ingredients I don't know
- [ ] Provenance/country of origin
- [ ] Locally sourced
- [ ] Welfare credentials (e.g. free-range or pasture-fed)
- [ ] Sustainability/carbon footprint
- [ ] Ethical sourcing (e.g. Fairtrade)
- [ ] Packaging (e.g. recyclable, plastic-free)
- [ ] Vegan or vegetarian
- [ ] Other (specify) _____

CHALLENGING FOOD DOGMA

Q2. Of those, which ONE is the most important to you?

- [ ] Taste/flavour
- [ ] Texture
- [ ] Price/affordability
- [ ] A food I like
- [ ] A food my family likes
- [ ] Calorie content
- [ ] Macros (protein, fat or carb content/ratio)
- [ ] Micros (vitamins, minerals, antioxidants, fibre etc)
- [ ] Functional properties (e.g. helps digestion, boosts energy)
- [ ] General healthfulness
- [ ] Fits into my meal plan
- [ ] Fits into the diet I follow (e.g. paleo, low-carb)
- [ ] Familiarity — whether I've tried it before
- [ ] Novelty/innovation — whether it's something new
- [ ] Convenience — easy to prepare/eat
- [ ] Seen it online/on social media
- [ ] Used/endorsed by celebrities
- [ ] Something I have a recipe for
- [ ] Brand/manufacturer
- [ ] Level of processing
- [ ] Number of ingredients
- [ ] Clean labelling
- [ ] No ingredients I don't know
- [ ] Provenance/country of origin
- [ ] Locally sourced
- [ ] Welfare credentials (e.g. free-range or pasture-fed)
- [ ] Sustainability/carbon footprint
- [ ] Ethical sourcing (e.g. Fairtrade)
- [ ] Packaging (e.g. recyclable, plastic-free)
- [ ] Vegan or vegetarian
- [ ] Other (specify) _____

Q3. How much of the food you eat has the characteristic you picked in Q2?

- [ ] All of it
- [ ] The vast majority
- [ ] About half
- [ ] About a quarter
- [ ] Less than a quarter
- [ ] None

CHALLENGING FOOD DOGMA

Q4. When you eat food that doesn't have the characteristics that matter to you, what is the most common reason why?

☐ Affordability — the food I'd ideally like to eat is too expensive

☐ Accessibility — can't always buy it where I live

☐ Convenience — don't always have time to buy and prepare it

☐ It clashes with what my family would like to eat

☐ Binges

☐ Boredom — don't always want to eat the same thing

☐ Lack of self-discipline — can't always stick to what I think I should be eating

☐ Other (specify) _____

Q5. How do you feel when you eat something that doesn't meet the characteristics you identified in Q1 and Q2?

☐ Very bad

☐ Fairly bad

☐ Doesn't really affect how I feel

Q6. Still thinking about the characteristics that matter to you when buying and eating food, would you say…?

☐ They're pretty much in line with what most people care about

☐ They're perhaps a little different to most people

☐ They're very different to what most people care about

Q7. Which of these statements do you agree with?

☐ I often feel judged for my food choices

☐ I sometimes feel other people judge me

☐ I don't think other people judge my food choices

Q8. What do you believe other people think about your food choices and the way you eat?

☐ Healthy

☐ Unhealthy

☐ Restrictive

☐ Erratic

☐ Excessive

☐ Not enough

☐ Faddish — driven by fad diets

☐ Weird

☐ At odds with what I look like

☐ I don't believe other people spend time thinking about how I eat

☐ Other (specify) _____

CHALLENGING FOOD DOGMA

Q9. Think back to when you were growing up and name three food rules your family had. This could be something like 'No one leaves the table until everybody is finished' or 'No meat on Fridays'.

Rule 1 ... _____

Rule 2 ... _____

Rule 3 ... _____

Q10. Looking back at these rules, do you now view them as….
- ☐ Very sensible and healthy
- ☐ Fairly sensible and healthy
- ☐ Not very sensible or healthy
- ☐ Not at all sensible or healthy

Q11. To what extent do you still stick to these rules?
- ☐ All the time
- ☐ Sometimes
- ☐ Not very often
- ☐ Not at all

Q12. When you were growing up, were you ever shamed for your food choices and eating habits?
- ☐ All the time
- ☐ Occasionally
- ☐ Not very often
- ☐ Not at all

Q13. If you were ever shamed, what were you shamed for?
- ☐ Eating too much
- ☐ Eating unhealthy foods (e.g. sweets)
- ☐ Eating someone else's foods
- ☐ Not eating enough
- ☐ Other (specify) _____

Q14. What impact has this had on your long-term eating habits?
- ☐ It's affected them a lot
- ☐ It's affected them a little
- ☐ It's not affected them very much
- ☐ It hasn't affected them at all

CHALLENGING FOOD DOGMA

Q15. Which of these statements describes how you feel about your eating habits today?

- ☐ My eating habits are the number one thing I'd like to change about my life
- ☐ I feel guilty about my eating habits a lot
- ☐ I'm mostly okay with them, but there are a few things I'd like to change
- ☐ I don't really think about my eating habits

Q16. Have you ever done any of the following?

- ☐ Tracked calories
- ☐ Tracked macros
- ☐ Kept a daily food log or diary
- ☐ Weighed your food or ingredients
- ☐ Checked the label for calories or nutritional information

Q17. In the past month, have you done any of the following?

- ☐ Tracked calories
- ☐ Tracked macros
- ☐ Kept a daily food log or diary
- ☐ Weighed your food or ingredients
- ☐ Checked the label for calories or nutritional information

Q18. Which of these statements do you agree with?

- ☐ Without daily checking and tracking, my eating would be completely out of control
- ☐ I need a degree of tracking to makes sure my eating habits are in line with my goals
- ☐ I don't do as much tracking and checking as I should
- ☐ I'd like to track my eating more, but I know it's not a healthy habit for me
- ☐ I don't track and check at all, and I'm happy that way

Q19. Sum up the three most important rules that govern your eating habits today. This could be something like 'I weigh everything I eat' or 'I choose pasture-fed meat whenever possible.'

Rule 1: ... _____

Rule 2: ... _____

Rule 3: ... _____

CHALLENGING FOOD DOGMA

Q20. What could you do to challenge and break these rules occasionally? (Write down as much detail as possible.)

_____

_____

_____

_____

_____

_____

_____

Q21. What are your main worries about breaking your food rules? What do you fear the consequences might be? (Write down as much detail as possible.)

_____

_____

_____

_____

_____

_____

_____

Q22. Now imagine how breaking your food rules could have a positive impact on your life. What do you think the benefits could be? (Give as much detail as possible.)

_____

_____

_____

_____

_____

_____

MOVING ON AFTER A SETBACK

Setbacks are an unavoidable aspect of recovery. but they don't have to derail your progress. Use the following questions and processes to help clarify why the setback happened. what you can learn from it — and how to move on decisively.

PART 1: WHAT HAPPENED?

Date: _____

Time of day: _____

Location: _____

Amount of money spent (if applicable): _____

Briefly describe what happened: ...

_____

_____

_____

Q1. How were you feeling at the time? (Give as much detail as possible.)

_____

_____

_____

_____

_____

Q2. Which of the following applied to you at the time?

- ☐ Bored/nothing to do
- ☐ Feeling lonely
- ☐ Feeling sick/rundown
- ☐ Unexpectedly had time to yourself
- ☐ Higher workload than usual
- ☐ Looming deadlines
- ☐ Had conflict/an argument with a family member
- ☐ Had conflict/an argument at work
- ☐ An important project went wrong
- ☐ An important project was completed/went well
- ☐ Sickness within the family
- ☐ Felt bad about your body or weight

MOVING ON AFTER A SETBACK

- [ ] Weighed yourself that day
- [ ] Went shopping for clothes/tried on clothes
- [ ] Deliberately tried to eat less than usual
- [ ] Deliberately tried to eat different foods than usual
- [ ] Had to have a meal outside of your usual routine (e.g. a lunch with a work contact)
- [ ] Ate something unplanned
- [ ] Someone commented on your weight (positive or negative)
- [ ] Someone tried to engage you in a conversation about body weight or dieting
- [ ] You were planning to have sex/be intimate with your partner later that day
- [ ] You were about to have your period

Q3. At the time, did you feel you had a good reason for binging?
- [ ] Yes
- [ ] No

Q3a. If so, what was your reason?
- [ ] I deserved a break
- [ ] I needed a way to unwind/de-stress
- [ ] I wasn't making much progress anyway
- [ ] I wanted to test myself and see if I could resist it
- [ ] I was fed up sticking to my self-help programme/following my therapist's advice
- [ ] I always binge when I'm on my period
- [ ] Other (specify) _____

Q4. Did you do any of the following afterwards?
- [ ] Purged/made yourself vomit
- [ ] Took laxatives
- [ ] Exercised
- [ ] Drank unusually large amounts of water

MOVING ON AFTER A SETBACK

PART 2: LEARNING LESSONS

Q5. How do you feel about what happened now? (Give as much detail as possible.)

_____

_____

_____

_____

_____

_____

_____

_____

Q6. Which of these statements do you agree with?

☐ I am completely surprised this happened — things were going well

☐ I knew this was coming

☐ I am devastated and don't think I can forgive myself

☐ This just proves that I will never get better

☐ I am annoyed, but ready to move on

Q7. Think of three things you could have done differently at the time.

1. _____

2. _____

3. _____

Q8. Might any of the following have made a difference?

☐ Calling, texting or speaking to someone

☐ Using a positive cue, affirmation or mantra

☐ Reminding yourself of your recovery goals/why you're doing this

☐ Knowing how bad you'd feel afterwards

☐ Going for a walk/exercising

☐ Having something to do

☐ Having an important appointment later that day

☐ Reading a book

☐ Listening to music

MOVING ON AFTER A SETBACK

Q9. Finish each sentence.

What disappoints me most about this setback is...

_____

_____

_____

The biggest lesson I've learned from this is... _____

_____

_____

One change I am making today to help prevent this in the future is... _____

_____

_____

_____

PART 3: MOVING ON

Q10. List the three most important reasons why you want to recover from binge eating.

Reason 1: ... _____

_____

Reason 2: ... _____

_____

Reason 3 .... _____

_____

Now make the following pledge, and date and sign it.

☐ What's done is done
☐ I've learned my lesson
☐ This setback doesn't define who I am or undo the progress I've made
☐ I have a whole year to get this right
☐ I forgive myself and promise not to punish myself
☐ I am drawing a line
☐ I'm ready to focus on what's next   /   /   [SIGNATURE]

SELF-HELP CHECKLIST

Use this worksheet to help structure your thinking about any self-help programme you are looking to follow, define goals and monitor your progress.

Name of the book or programme: _____

Author: _____

Q1. What made you pick this book/programme?
☐ Saw it mentioned online
☐ Word of mouth recommendation
☐ A doctor/therapist or coach recommended it
☐ Good reviews
☐ Liked the title/blurb
☐ Seems different/a new approach
☐ Author seems credible
☐ Have read other titles by the same author
☐ No specific reason — just appealed to me

Q2. What are your hopes and expectations for this book?
☐ I will stop binging
☐ I will binge less than I currently do
☐ I might still binge but it'll have less of an impact on my life
☐ I will learn to love and accept myself
☐ I will stop feeling so bad about my body
☐ I will lose weight
☐ I will gain a new perspective on binge eating
☐ I will get some useful advice I can incorporate in my recovery
☐ Other (specify) _____

Q3. Based on everything you've learned about the recovery process, are your expectations realistic? How might you make them more realistic? (Give as much detail as possible.)

_____

_____

_____

_____

_____

SELF-HELP CHECKLIST

Q4. In your own words, what are you hoping to learn as a result of reading this book? (Give as much detail as possible.)

_____

_____

_____

_____

_____

FIRST READING

Start by reading the whole book first. Don't do any of the exercises at this stage - just let the book sink in.

Q5. What are your first impressions having read the book?

☐ It's just as I thought it would be

☐ It's different to what I expected — in a good way

☐ It's different to what I expected — in a bad way

Q6. If the book is different to what you expected, describe how. (Provide as much detail as possible.)

_____

_____

_____

_____

Q7. Do you still believe the book is worth continuing with?

☐ Yes

☐ No

Q8. If not, what are you going to do next? (Provide as much detail as possible.)

_____

_____

_____

_____

SELF-HELP CHECKLIST

Q9. If you are continuing with the book, what are you most excited about trying? (Be as specific as possible.)

_____

_____

_____

_____

_____

Q10. Is there anything in the book that you are unsure or worried about at this stage? (Again, be specific.)

_____

_____

_____

_____

TAKING ACTION

Now read the book again, this time noting down the main actions it requires you to take. Try to be as specific as possible.

Action 1: _____

Action 2: _____

Action 3: _____

Action 4: _____

Action 5: _____

SELF-HELP CHECKLIST

Action 6: _____

_____

Action 7: _____

_____

Action 8: _____

_____

Action 9: _____

_____

Action 10: _____

_____

Q11. Do you need to buy anything or make preparations before you are able to take the actions described in the book?

☐ Yes
☐ No

Q12. If yes, what do you need to buy or prepare? (Provide as much detail as possible.)

_____

_____

_____

_____

_____

_____

_____

_____

_____

_____

Q13. When will you start to implement the actions? (Please specify a date.)   ___ / ___ / ___

SELF-HELP CHECKLIST

MONITORING PROGRESS

This is where you define how you are going to monitor your progress. Use the separate Weekly Review Sheet to track and review progress on a weekly basis.

Q14. How will you decide if the book/programme is working for you? (Be as specific as possible?)

_____

_____

_____

_____

_____

_____

_____

_____

Q15. What kinds of positive food behaviours do you want to see in your life as a result of the book/programme? (Again, please be specific.)

_____

_____

_____

_____

_____

_____

_____

_____

_____

_____

_____

_____

SELF-HELP CHECKLIST

Q16. And what kinds of positive non-food behaviours do you want to see? (Be specific.)

_____

_____

_____

_____

_____

_____

_____

_____

_____

Q17. What would you consider red flags or warning signs to tell you the book/programme is harming you and should be stopped? (Think about this carefully and provide as much detail as possible.)

_____

_____

_____

_____

_____

_____

_____

_____

_____

_____

NEW THERAPIST CHECKLIST

Use this checklist to help guide you when considering a new therapist, coach or counsellor.

STEP 1: THE BASICS

Name of the therapist or coach: _____

Type of therapy or coaching style they specialise in: _____

Q1. Which of the following best describes the level of their qualifications?

☐ PhD/doctor
☐ University degree (specify which discipline) _____
☐ Diploma (specify exact name) _____
☐ Other professional qualification (specify exact name) _____
☐ Informal training
☐ No professional or formal qualification
☐ Not sure

Q2. Which institution awarded their qualification? _____

Q3. How long did they have to study for their qualification?

☐ 5+ years
☐ 3–5 years
☐ 1–3 years
☐ Less than one year
☐ Not sure

Q4. Which professional bodies are they registered with? _____

Q5. Which of the following best describes them?

☐ They specialise in dealing with binge eating problems
☐ They deal with a range of eating disorders, including binge eating
☐ They are a general counsellor or coach, with no specific focus on binge eating

Q6. How you did you hear about this therapist or coach?

☐ Referral by a doctor, nurse or GP
☐ Recommendation by a friend or family member
☐ Recommendation/referral by an eating disorder charity/organisation
☐ Internet search
☐ Online groups or forums
☐ Other (specify) _____

NEW THERAPIST CHECKLIST

Q7. Was it your decision to start seeing a therapist or coach?

☐ Yes, entirely mine

☐ Someone else suggested it, but I agree it's a good idea

☐ Not my decision — someone else wants me to do this

STEP 2: UNDERSTANDING WHAT TO EXPECT

Q8. How many sessions do you have to commit to? _____

Q9. How much will you have to pay for each session? _____

Q10. Have you been offered a trial session?

☐ Yes, and I'm taking it

☐ Yes, but I turned it down

☐ I asked for one, but they said no

☐ Wasn't offered and didn't ask

Q11. Do you understand how each session will be structured and what it will involve?

☐ I have a very clear idea

☐ I have a good idea

☐ I am not really sure

☐ I have no idea

Q12. Will you be given homework or assignments to do outside of sessions?

☐ Yes

☐ No

☐ Not sure

Q13. How much time will these out-of-session assignments likely take up every day and week?

_____

Q14. What does the therapist/coach say happens with most of their binge eating clients?

☐ They are completely cured

☐ They make considerable improvement

☐ They make some improvement

☐ Their binging doesn't necessarily improve, but they're happier/have better coping skills

☐ Other (specify) _____

NEW THERAPIST CHECKLIST

Q15. And what did they say should be your expectations for your own recovery? (Provide as much detail as possible.)

_____

_____

_____

_____

Q16. How long, on average, does it take for their clients to achieve the outcome described at Q14?

- [ ] Less than three months
- [ ] 3-6 months
- [ ] 6 months to a year
- [ ] More than one year

Q17. How credible do you think this is?

- [ ] Very credible
- [ ] Somewhat credible
- [ ] Not very credible
- [ ] Not at all credible
- [ ] Not sure

STEP 3: TAKING STOCK

Q18. Overall, would you say this therapist or coach is....

- [ ] Exactly the kind of person I was hoping to see
- [ ] Not exactly what I was hoping for, but a pretty good match
- [ ] Not really the kind of person I was hoping to see

Q19. If this person isn't a perfect match, why is that?

- [ ] Doesn't offer the type of therapy I want
- [ ] Doesn't have the level of qualifications I'd ideally want
- [ ] Doesn't live as close to me as I would like — have to travel to see them
- [ ] More expensive than I would like/can afford
- [ ] Not someone I can see in person — sessions will by online or via telephone
- [ ] Not my choice — someone else has picked the person for me
- [ ] Other (specify) _____

NEW THERAPIST CHECKLIST

Q20. How comfortable do you feel asking questions of the therapist or coach?

☐ Very comfortable — they seem open and happy to answer questions

☐ Fairly comfortable

☐ Not very comfortable

☐ Not at all comfortable

Q21. If you don't feel comfortable, why is this?

☐ I feel awkward/don't like asking challenging questions

☐ It'll make me look like I'm not committed/ready for therapy

☐ They seemed reluctant to answer the questions I had

☐ They are an expert/very highly qualified — don't feel it's my place to question them

☐ Don't think they would take it well

☐ Other (specify) _____

Q22. Overall, do you feel…?

☐ Very happy to start sessions with them

☐ Quite happy to start sessions with them

☐ Not particularly happy to start sessions with them

☐ Not at all happy to start sessions with them

Q23. If you aren't happy, what are your next steps?

☐ Try them for a few sessions and see how it goes

☐ Look for someone else

☐ Not do therapy/coaching for the time being

Q24. Write down any other questions, thoughts or reflections you have.

_____

_____

_____

_____

_____

_____

_____

_____

WEEKLY RECOVERY REVIEW

Week start date: _____

End date: _____

This is recovery week number: _____

PART 1: REVIEW

Q1. What were the main goals you were hoping to achieve this past week, and how well did you do? Score each goal from 1 to 5. where 1 = didn't meet my goal at all and 5 = met my goal completely.

Food-related goals

Goal 1: _____

Score: ① ② ③ ④ ⑤

Goal 2: _____

Score: ① ② ③ ④ ⑤

Goal 3: _____

Score: ① ② ③ ④ ⑤

Goal 4: _____

Score: ① ② ③ ④ ⑤

Goal 5: _____

Score: ① ② ③ ④ ⑤

WEEKLY RECOVERY REVIEW

Non-food goals

Goal 1: _____

Score: ① ② ③ ④ ⑤

Goal 2: _____

Score: ① ② ③ ④ ⑤

Goal 3: _____

Score: ① ② ③ ④ ⑤

Goal 4: _____

Score: ① ② ③ ④ ⑤

Goal 5: _____

Score: ① ② ③ ④ ⑤

Q2. Overall, how did you do with your recovery this past week?
- ☐ Very well
- ☐ Fairly well
- ☐ Not very well
- ☐ Not at all well

Q3. What was your biggest achievement this past week? (Provide as much detail as possible.)

_____

_____

_____

_____

WEEKLY RECOVERY REVIEW

Q4. Did any of the following apply to you?

☐ I continued working on my recovery despite a setback

☐ I continued working on my recovery despite not always feeling motivated

☐ I binged and then got back on track

☐ I resisted weighing myself

☐ I made time for journaling and reflection

☐ I made an effort to spend less time thinking about food

☐ I opened up to someone about my binge eating

☐ Other (specify) _____

Q5. What was your biggest setback or disappointment this past week? (Provide as much detail as possible.)

_____

_____

_____

Q6. What did this teach you? (Again, be as specific as possible.)

_____

_____

_____

Q7. What will you do differently in the coming week as a result? (Be specific.)

_____

_____

_____

Q8. What have you done in the past week to look after yourself or be kind to yourself? (Provide as much detail as you can.)

_____

_____

_____

WEEKLY RECOVERY REVIEW

PART 2: LOOKING AHEAD

Q9. What are your main goals for the coming week?

Food-related goals

Goal 1: _____

Goal 2: _____

Goal 3: _____

Goal 4: _____

Goal 5: _____

Non-food goals

Goal 1: _____

Goal 2: _____

Goal 3: _____

Goal 4: _____

Goal 5: _____

Q10. Run a quick sense-check on your goals. Are they all...?
- [ ] Specific
- [ ] Realistic
- [ ] Action-focused
- [ ] Unrelated to your weight or body shape

Q11. Overall, how confident are you about achieving your goals for next week?
- [ ] Very confident
- [ ] Fairly confident
- [ ] Not very confident
- [ ] Not at all confident

WEEKLY RECOVERY REVIEW

Q12. What would help you feel more confident in your ability to meet your goals? (Be as specific as possible.)

_____

_____

Q13. What are you hoping to learn about yourself in the coming week? (Again, provide as much detail as you can.)

_____

_____

Q14. What, if anything, are you worried about in the week ahead? (Be specific.)

_____

_____

Q15. Are there any appointments, social engagements or other events that you might find challenging next week? (Provide as much detail as possible.)

_____

_____

Q16. What can you do to better cope with these? (Write down as much detail as possible.)

_____

_____

Q17. What will you do for self-care or to show kindness to yourself next week? (Be specific.)

_____

_____

Q18. Write down any other thoughts or observations about the past week or the week ahead.

_____

_____

_____

_____

MONTHLY RECOVERY REVIEW

Use this in combination with the Monthly Recovery Goal Tracker and your Weekly Recovery Review Sheets to keep tabs on how you are progressing and set goals for the month ahead.

Month: _____

This is month number _____ **of my recovery year.**

PART 1: REVIEW

Q1. What were the main goals you were hoping to achieve in the past month, and how well did you do?
Score each goal from 1 to 5, where 1 = didn't meet my goal at all and 5 = met my goal completely.

Food-related goals

Goal 1: _____

Score: ① ② ③ ④ ⑤

Goal 2: _____

Score: ① ② ③ ④ ⑤

Goal 3: _____

Score: ① ② ③ ④ ⑤

Goal 4: _____

Score: ① ② ③ ④ ⑤

Goal 5: _____

Score: ① ② ③ ④ ⑤

MONTHLY RECOVERY REVIEW

Non-food goals

Goal 1: _____

Score: ① ② ③ ④ ⑤

Goal 2: _____

Score: ① ② ③ ④ ⑤

Goal 3: _____

Score: ① ② ③ ④ ⑤

Goal 4: _____

Score: ① ② ③ ④ ⑤

Goal 5: _____

Score: ① ② ③ ④ ⑤

Q2. Overall, how did you do with your recovery this past month?
☐ Very well
☐ Fairly well
☐ Not very well
☐ Not at all well

Q3. What was your biggest achievement this past month? (Provide as much detail as possible.)

_____

_____

_____

_____

MONTHLY RECOVERY REVIEW

Q4. What was your biggest setback or disappointment? (Provide as much detail as possible.)

_____

_____

_____

Q5. What's the main thing you learned this month? (Again, be as specific as possible.)

_____

_____

_____

PART 2: LOOKING AHEAD

Q6. What are your main goals for next month?

Food-related goals

Goal 1: _____

Goal 2: _____

Goal 3: _____

Goal 4: _____

Goal 5: _____

MONTHLY RECOVERY REVIEW

Non-food goals

Goal 1: _____

Goal 2: _____

Goal 3: _____

Goal 4: _____

Goal 5: _____

Q7. Are all your goals….?
- [ ] Specific
- [ ] Realistic
- [ ] Action-focused
- [ ] Unrelated to your weight or body shape

Q8. Overall, how confident are you about achieving your goals for next month?
- [ ] Very confident
- [ ] Fairly confident
- [ ] Not very confident
- [ ] Not at all confident

Q9. What would help you feel more confident in your ability to meet your goals? (Provide as much detail as possible.)

_____

_____

_____

Q10. What are you hoping to learn about yourself in the coming month? (Be as specific as possible.)

_____

_____

_____

_____

MONTHLY RECOVERY REVIEW

Q11. What, if anything, are you worried about in the month ahead? (Be as specific as possible.)

_____

_____

_____

Q12. Are there any appointments, social engagements or other events that you might find challenging next month? (Provide as much detail as possible.)

_____

_____

_____

Q13. What can you do to better cope with these? (Be specific.)

_____

_____

_____

PART 3: RECOMMIT

Read and sign the following pledge.

I, _____ hereby recommit myself to another month of recovery.

I know it won't be easy, but I am determined to do what's needed to get better.

I promise to work hard.
I promise to hold myself accountable.
I promise not to be thrown off course by setback.
I promise to look after myself and practice kindness and forgiveness towards myself.
Most importantly, I promise to keep going no matter what.

I am ready for another month.

SIGNATURE

YOUR RECOVERY PLEDGE

Date and sign this pledge to mark the official start of your recovery year.

I, _____ _____ hereby pledge the following:

That I will give myself a full year to work on my recovery from binge eating, starting ___ / ___ / ___

That I will approach my recovery year in the spirit of openness and learning

That I will try out different ideas and recovery techniques, even if they push me out of my comfort zone

That I will give each new idea a fair chance before deciding it it's right for me

That I will hold myself accountable by keeping a regular record of my thoughts, feelings and progress in my recovery journal

That I will make time to look after myself

That I will keep a close eye on negative self-talk and attempts at self-sabotage

That I will aim for progress over perfection

That I will recognise my achievements and celebrate my recovery milestones

That I accept recovery is hard work, and this is going to take my best effort

That I will resist snake oil merchants promising me miracle cures or an easy way out

That I will use my critical faculties and keep educating myself about binge eating

That I will not attempt to diet or lose weight during my recovery year

That I accept setbacks are part of the process

That I will practice kindness and forgiveness towards myself when those setbacks happen

That I won't attempt to do this alone and instead commit to speaking to someone about my binge eating

That I will keep going, no matter what

SIGNATURE

RECOVERY GOALS TRACKER

Use this worksheet to log and track your recovery goals on a monthly basis.
Each goal has a 31-day tracker next to it – if your goal isn't daily but, say, weekly, tick off only one day each week and leave the rest blank.

MY 5 FOOD-RELATED RECOVERY GOALS

Goal 1 _____

Goal 2 _____

Goal 3 _____

Goal 4 _____

Goal 5 _____

MY 5 NON-FOOD RECOVERY GOALS

Goal 1 _____

Goal 2 _____

Goal 3 _____

Goal 4 _____

Goal 5 _____

AFTERWORD

And here we are. I hope my book and my story have helped you look at your binge eating in a new light and given you fresh ideas and inspiration for how to tackle it.

Above all, I hope they have given you renewed confidence that recovery is possible — even for you. Binge eating doesn't have to define your life. If you are willing to work hard at it — and willing to swap wishful thinking for real-life improvement — then it's a problem that absolutely can be beaten. You can beat it. Perhaps not as quickly as you'd like. Perhaps not as neatly as you'd like. But you can beat it.

I wish you great strength and courage for your journey.

Keep In Touch

I blog and post updates at www.bingeeatingrecoveryproject.com and send occasional updates on my own journey — as well as anything related to this book — via my reader newsletter.

You can sign up at:

www.bingeeatingrecoveryproject.com/readernewsletter

Help Others Discover This Book

Finally, if you enjoyed this book, I have a quick favour to ask: Please consider spending a few minutes to leave an honest review on Amazon.

Reviews make a huge difference to independently published books like this, and help other readers discover titles that could be helpful for them.

Thank you so much.

USEFUL CONTACTS

Australia
Butterfly Foundation for Eating Disorders
www.thebutterflyfoundation.org.au

Canada
National Eating Disorder Information Service (NEDIC)
www.nedic.ca

Ireland
Bodywhys
www.bodywhys.ie

New Zealand
EDANZ
www.ed.org.nz

United Kingdom
BEAT
www.beateatingdisorders.org.uk

USA
National Eating Disorders Association (NEDA)
www.nationaleatingdisorders.org

For a more comprehensive list, including organisations in non-English speaking countries, Mirror-Mirror have a helpful overview at www.mirror-mirror.org/natorg.htm

Made in the USA
Monee, IL
06 December 2019